THE FREUD ANNIVERSARY
LECTURE SERIES
THE NEW YORK PSYCHOANALYTIC
INSTITUTE

THE FREUD ANNIVERSARY LECTURE SERIES

The New York Psychoanalytic Institute

PSYCHOANALYTIC AVENUES TO ART

Robert Waelder, Ph.D.

INTERNATIONAL UNIVERSITIES PRESS, INC.

New York

This is an expanded version of the Lecture
given at The New York Academy of Medicine
on May 21, 1963.

Contents

List of Illustrations

Part I

Aspects of Aesthetic Response

Introduction

What Is Beauty?

IT IS NOT easy to describe the nature of beauty in psychoanalytic terms. Scientific models hardly ever work equally well in all areas of reality. To expect that they do, or ever could, is one of the countless illusions to which the human mind is prone and to which it clings as long as possible and often a good deal longer. In fact, the best scientific models mirror reality well in certain areas for which they have been designed, less well in adjacent areas, and perhaps not at all in others. The psychoanalytic model, with its concepts of instinctual drives, danger signals, and ego mechanisms, has evolved in the study of psychopathology and of character formation; it is plainly indispensable in these areas and in the study of inner conflict in general. It is less relevant in conflict-free areas.

Art seems to extend from an area full of conflict, often beset by inner storms, into one of calm which seems to be fairly free of conflict. The tragic sense of life that permeates the later work of Rembrandt and the exuberance of a happy and not visibly neurotic man like Rubens who warmed both hands at the fires of life are examples from the two ends of the spectrum. Rembrandt's later works reveal a personality and a view of life that has deepened under the impact of suffering; the works of Rubens seem to address themselves, as the dedication to Stendhal's *Charterhouse of Parma* says, "to the happy few."

The experience of beauty is probably originally a sensual experience but one that is less intense in terms of physical excitement than are sexual experiences which are related to the erotogenic zones in the narrow sense of the word. Perhaps one could speak of *subacute sexuality*, of a sensation on the periphery of the sexual. Augustine speaks in one breath of *concupiscentia carnis, concupiscentia oculorum et ambitio saeculi*—the greed of the flesh, the greed of the eyes, and secular ambition. The enjoyment of beauty is perhaps the satisfaction of the greed of the eyes (and, one may add, of the ears and the other senses as well).

One is tempted to say that here we are dealing with desexualized, or neutralized, energies. Such concepts have their legitimate place where a sexual interest has decreased or disappeared and an interest of nonsexual, or less manifestly sexual, character has arisen; for in such cases we may think of the latter as being a substitute for the former. But

[12]

where there is no previous history of a corresponding decline of an overtly sexual interest—as, for instance, there is no such previous history of the apparent enjoyment of a tune by a one-year-old child—reference to "neutralized" or "neutral" energies does not seem to add anything to the description of the phenomenon; in such cases, the term is redundant rather than explanatory.

The Beauty of Natural Objects and the Beauty of Artifacts

We distinguish the beauty of natural objects from the beauty of man-made artifacts. A photograph of a beautiful woman is not necessarily beautiful as a work of art, even though it may convey the beauty of the sitter. The rendering of things that are unattractive and even repellent may be beautiful in terms of art.

The most horrible has at times been presented by art, in word or picture, in a way in which we feel an aesthetic quality, though we may sometimes hesitate to apply the word, beauty, to it and prefer other terms of appreciation instead. Ugolino's story, told to Dante in Hell, of his and his sons' slow death by starvation and his chilling, implacable hatred of his jailer, Archbishop Ruggieri; Euripides's Medea, who slaughters her own children almost on the stage to revenge herself on Jason for his faithlessness; or Grünewald's Cruci-

[13]

fixion are famous examples. Velasquez's painting of a feeble-minded dwarf belongs to the glories of pictorial art although the sitter cannot be called beautiful.

There are many ways in which the description of something that is ugly in reality can yet be beautiful, and the following anecdote may illustrate one of them. A book on *The Nature of Politics,* recently published, seemed outstanding to me, and I wrote to the author to tell him how much I had enjoyed it. He replied that he had not expected anyone would describe his book as a joy. The author and I were obviously talking of different things; he, no doubt facetiously, referred to the facts described in his book—facts which indeed gave no reason for joy—while I had in mind the depth in which these realities had been grasped and the lucidity with which they had been presented.

We must add, however, that in the visual arts, though the beauty of artifacts can be distinguished from the beauty of nature, the former is in practice *hardly ever entirely independent* of the latter. Most of the time, we appreciate a work of art more if, other things being equal, the objects represented or suggested are beautiful as well. A painting of a beautiful young woman is usually more sought after than one of an ugly hag. Two seascapes by Charles Brooking, of approximately the same size and reputedly of comparable quality, one

[14]

representing a pleasant scene, the other a ship-wreck, were recently sold in Christie's auction rooms at prices differing in a ratio of more than 10:1.[1] It is hard to believe that there are many collectors who would hang Rembrandt's carcass of an ox in their living rooms, however much they may appreciate the quality of the painting.

What follows is an attempt to discuss the impact of art from a psychoanalytic point of view: to review the basic analytic contributions and to examine the scope of their application and their possible generalizations. I shall begin with the consideration of phenomena which occur before the differentiation of the mind into an id and an ego, or for which this distinction is not relevant. I shall then proceed, roughly, though not always exactly, to consider the id, ego, and superego aspects respectively.

[1] One may wonder, of course, whether prices are an adequate measure of the current appreciation of a work of art. But what is? Prices are the result of a plebiscite in which only those vote who are willing and able to back up their preferences with their cash and in which each has as many votes as he has dollars to spend. The "electorate" includes professional art critics who operate as museum directors or as advisors to private collectors as well as assorted men of means of varying backgrounds.

1. Basic Considerations

...Καὶ ἔστιν αὖ μουσικὴ περὶ ἁρμονίαν
καὶ ῥυθμὸν ἐρωτικῶν ἐπιστήμη.

... moreover, music is knowledge of
the erotic qualities of harmony and
rhythm.

—PLATO

The Beauty of Configurations

Perhaps the simplest form of beauty, a kind of
subcerebral stratum in the realm of beauty, is that
of certain configurations or Gestalten—pleasing arrangements of colors and shapes, or of sounds or of
their sequence in time. Such configurations can
probably be studied from more than one point of
view. One possible approach is to see them as *patterns of tension and discharge*—either distributed
in space as configurations of line, volume, light
and shade, or color, or distributed in time, as in
a sequence of tones and harmonies. *If* we approach
them in this way, psychoanalytic categories become applicable.

Psychoanalysis has tried to see pleasure as a

function of tensions, and thus to see a psychic sensation as a function of physiological processes; and while there is as yet no satisfactory psychoanalytic theory along these lines, there are some important experiences and preliminary considerations. In Kantian language, we may speak of *Prolegomena* to a future psychophysiological theory of pleasure, of which a brief review will be attempted in what follows.

Pleasure as Function of Tension and Discharge

In his attempt to see the subjective sensation of pleasure as a function of the "objective" fact of tension which, at least in principle, is subject to intersubjective verification, Freud thought at first that "a feeling of tension necessarily involves unpleasure" (1905a, p. 209). He apparently looked at the monumental examples of the great appetites, hunger, thirst, and the desire for copulation, all pressing toward satiation.

But, on the other hand, there was also the patent fact that, except for a very high level of tension, pleasure is felt not only in the final satisfaction which reduces the tensions to zero but also, to a degree, in the state of tension and in the mounting of tension, somewhat as it is implied in the lines in Goethe's *Faust:*

Thus I reel from desire to enjoyment
And in enjoyment languish for desire.

[17]

Freud tried to give account of this situation by distinguishing between forepleasure and end pleasure, the former accompanying the "appropriate" stimulation of an erotogenic zone and moderate in degree, the latter "brought about entirely by discharge" and "highest in intensity" (1905a, p. 210).

These considerations did not answer the question whether or not, or how, forepleasure could be made a special case of a general theory which describes pleasure of all kinds as a function of tension. At a later time, and with a view toward developing such a general theory, Freud suggested that the *rate of change* may be the decisive factor:

> We have decided to relate pleasure and unpleasure to the quantity of excitation that is present in the mind but is not in any way 'bound'; and to relate them in such a manner that unpleasure corresponds to an *increase* in the quantity of excitation and pleasure to a *diminution*. What we are implying by this is not a simple relation between the strength of the feelings of pleasure and unpleasure and the corresponding modifications in the quantity of excitation; least of all —in view of all we have been taught by psychophysiology—are we suggesting a direct proportional ratio: the factor that determines the feeling is probably the amount of increase or diminution in the quantity of excitation *in a given period of time* [1920, p. 7f].

The same idea was repeated in the form of a question (1920, p. 63):

[18]

. . . is the feeling of tension to be related to the absolute magnitude, or perhaps to the level, of the cathexis, while the pleasure and unpleasure series indicates a change in the magnitude of the cathexis *within a given unit of time?*

These ideas reflect the influence of Fechner's logarithmic law of sensation. But Freud did not follow this course any further and finally decided that while it was correct to look for the conditions of pleasure and unpleasure in the time curve of tension, the *exact nature of this function was still unknown:*

> Pleasure and unpleasure . . . cannot be referred to an increase or decrease of a quantity (which we describe as 'tension due to stimulus'), although they obviously have a great deal to do with this factor. It appears that they depend, not on this quantitative factor, but on some characteristic of it which we can only describe as a qualitative one. If we were able to say what this qualitative characteristic is, we should be much further advanced in psychology. Perhaps it is the rhythm, the temporal sequence of changes, rises and falls in the quantity of stimulus. We do not know [1924, p. 160].

Thus, it appears likely that the sensation of pleasure and unpleasure is a function of tension and its changes in time, but we cannot give the exact formula of this function in general terms. We can, however, relate pleasure and unpleasure to

[19]

tension and its changes in individual instances. Moreover, whatever the exact form of the curve may be, we have reason to believe that its flexibility is limited, i.e., that minute differences in the tension curve can make the difference between pleasure and unpleasure, even intense unpleasure. There may be too little as well as too much stimulation. A French proverb says that there is only one step from the sublime to the ridiculous; one could equally say that there is only one step from pleasure to unpleasure through overexcitation or underexcitation.

This seems to apply not only to sexual pursuits on various levels but also to the "subacute" sensuality of beauty. The fifth-century Greek sculptor Polyclitus is credited with the remark that the quality of a work of art depends on many numerical relationships, with minimal amounts being decisive. Robert Browning expressed the same idea in the words:

Oh, the little more and how much it is!
And the little less and what worlds away!

The Development of Taste

Whatever the relationship of pleasure to tension may be, it is clear that it does not remain forever the same but changes with experience. In the very earliest infancy, pleasure seems to lie in the relief from tension alone. Thereafter, to an ever-increas-

[20]

ing extent, stimulations are not avoided but sought out; this is one of the facts that have led Freud to the formulation of a theory which sees life as a struggle between an expansive, tension-seeking life instinct and a restrictive, tension-reducing death instinct.

Whatever the pros and cons of the latter theory, it is unmistakable that, in the realm of the sexual instincts, longer and longer detours on the way to final satisfaction become pleasurable in the course of experience. In sexual life in the narrowest sense of the word, the more experienced adult tends both to prolong and to variegate forepleasure; in this largely consists the *ars amatoria,* the art of loving. The gastronome uses appetizers to whet his appetite; he avoids eating too much of one dish to keep his appetite alive for other courses, and avoids "filling" dishes altogether. While some nuclear desires remain essentially the same (though admitting of, and perhaps requiring, variety and refinement), others become stale through repetition and attract no more. The *speed of obsolescence,* i.e., the intensity of the need for new stimulation, *varies* enormously with individual and cultural conditions.

The basic pattern of the development of taste can also be seen in the change of the objects which exercise the strongest "sex appeal." Erotic publications which address themselves to adolescent boys or to uneducated adults contain photos of female nudes in which the sexual characteristics are in plain view and well emphasized. Publications geared to the educated consumer prefer understatement to emphasis, hint to direct statement, and a game of hide-and-seek to plain exposure. The originally most exciting parts of the female body are often not shown at all. They may be covered by a piece of clothing or a sheet which in reality could be easily removed or is about to fall; or, while not visible to the beholder of the picture, they might be visible to an observer located in another place, perhaps behind the plane of the picture; or they might lie outside the cut of the picture and be supplemented by the imagination of the beholder.

The development of taste is particularly obvious in music, where combinations that have been experienced as dissonant and could be tolerated only to a limited degree and only for a limited time have become more and more accepted, with resolution ever farther postponed or never to come at all. The major third was not accepted as a final accord in medieval music. There were still many music lovers in my childhood who were conditioned by the harmonies of Beethoven and Brahms and to whom the innovations of, for instance, Richard Strauss, were offensive. Since then, there have been several generations, each of which has introduced into music tonal configurations which would have been cacophonous to the preceding one.

In some cases, the development leads to an actual *reversal* of taste. The taste for the sweet, both in the literary and the figurative sense, which is general in childhood, is regularly replaced in adulthood by a taste for the tart, the bitter. The adult, as a rule, prefers wine to fruit juices, and habitués prefer dry to sweet wines.

This typical development may then secondarily produce a social valuation, and the taste for the tart and the bitter is taken as a mark of adulthood and of sophistication. The adolescent boy who tries his first smoke is often revolted by it, but he bravely carries on until he has learned, at first to tolerate, and then to like it.

2. An Id Approach:
A Preserve for the Pleasure Principle

> *Wenn du im Reich der Träume dich
> verweilet. . . .*
>
> If you dwelt in the realm of dreams....
> [Jupiter, speaking to the poet who
> appeared too late to the distribution
> of the earth and complained because
> there was nothing left any more.]
> —SCHILLER

Freud saw in art, above all, an opportunity for
the fulfillment, in fantasy, of wishes which in real
life are frustrated either by external obstacles or
by moral inhibitions. Art, then, is a kind of wild-
life preserve in the development from the pleasure
principle to the reality principle and serves as a
safety valve in civilization. Freud expressed himself on this subject several times, in similar terms,
and it seems indicated to quote his statements ex-
tensively in view of the fact that they have often
been misinterpreted:

Art brings about a reconciliation between the two principles [viz., the pleasure principle and the reality principle] in a peculiar way. An artist is originally a man who turns away from reality because he cannot come to terms with the renunciation of instinctual satisfaction which it at first demands, and who allows his erotic and ambitious wishes full play in the life of phantasy. He finds the way back to reality, however, from this world of phantasy by making use of special gifts to mould his phantasies into truths of a new kind, which are valued by men as precious reflections of reality. Thus in a certain fashion he actually becomes the hero, the king, the creator, or the favourite he desired to be, without following the long roundabout path of making real alterations in the external world. But he can only achieve this because other men feel the same dissatisfaction as he does with the renunciation demanded by reality, and because that dissatisfaction, which results from the replacement of the pleasure principle by the reality principle, is itself part of reality [1911, p. 224].

[And shortly thereafter:] In only a single field of our civilization has the omnipotence of thoughts been retained, and that is in the field of art. Only in art does it still happen that a man who is consumed by desires performs something resembling the accomplishment of those desires and that what he does in play produces emotional effects—thanks to artistic illusion—just as though it were something real [1913a, p. 90].

[And again:] . . . art . . . an activity intended to allay ungratified wishes—in the first place in the creative artist himself and subsequently in his audience or spectators. . . . The artist's first aim is to set himself free and, by communicating his work to other people suffering from the same arrested desires, he offers them the same liberation. He represents his most personal wishful phantasies as fulfilled; but they only become a work of art when they have undergone a transformation which *softens what is offensive in them, conceals their personal origin and, by obeying the laws of beauty, bribes other people with a bonus of pleasure.* Psycho-analysis has no difficulty in pointing out, alongside the *manifest part* of artistic enjoyment, another that is *latent though far more potent,* derived from hidden sources of instinctual liberation.

. . . Art is a conventionally accepted reality in which, thanks to artistic illusion, symbols and substitutes are able to provoke real emotions. Thus art constitutes a region half-way between a reality which frustrates wishes and the wish-fulfilling world of the imagination—a region in which, as it were, primitive man's strivings for omnipotence are still in full force [1913b, p. 187f.; italics added].

A decade later he returned to the same motifs:

The realm of imagination was seen to be a 'reservation' made during the painful transition from the pleasure principle to the reality principle in order to provide a substitute for instinctual satisfactions which had to be given up in real life. The artist, like the neurotic, had *withdrawn from an unsatisfactory reality into this world of imagination;* but, unlike the neurotic, *he knew how to find a way back from it* and once

[26]

more to get a firm foothold in reality. His creations, works of art, were the imaginary satisfactions of unconscious wishes, just as dreams are;
and like them they were in the nature of com-
promises, since they too were forced to avoid any
open conflict with the forces of repression. But
they differed from the asocial, narcissistic products of dreaming in that they were calculated to
arouse sympathetic interest in other people and
were able to evoke and to satisfy the same unconscious wishful impulses in them too. Besides this,
they made use of the perceptual pleasure of formal beauty as what I have called an 'incentive
bonus' [1925, p. 64f.; italics added].

Clearly, these lines were written with the arts of
the word—poetry, the drama, the novel—foremost
in mind, but they apply also to the nonverbal arts
in so far as the *literary content* or the literary associations of a work are concerned, or the memories
which it activates.

The theory suggests that, under certain conditions, products of the imagination can "represent
most personal wishes as fulfilled." Three cases must
be distinguished: the respective wishes may have
been ousted from consciousness (*repressed*) as dangerous, or *condemned* as sinful while yet conscious,
or merely *frustrated* by external obstacles. Freud's
conditions were formulated with the first two cases
foremost in mind; they are:

(a) that the goal of the drive be disguised and
in some degree modified;

[27]

(b) that the product has the merits of "formal beauty"; and

(c) that the expression of the fantasy is not a purely selfish matter, but that it is communicated to others with a view to its being enjoyed by them, too, and so becomes a social act.

There are also cases in which wishes are not forbidden but merely obstructed. In those cases, the work of art has to create the "artistic illusion"; and though the wishes are not subject to repression or moral condemnation, they often appear to the adult mind as childish dreams and as escapism of which a mature person has to be ashamed. This kind of censure must also be appeased by the merits of "formal beauty," by the fact that they are enjoyed in common, and sometimes also by modifications and disguises of the actual goal, although these will be less extensive than in the cases of desires reprehensible or repressed.

These cases may now be considered more closely.

(a) Repressed and Condemned Wishes

The first condition—modification and disguise of the goal—is reminiscent of the disguises under which a piece of subversive political writing can pass or outwit censorship, and of the distortions in dreams and in screen memories. The modification which makes the expression of a drive more acceptable has the form of desexualization, which

PSYCHOANALYTIC AVENUES TO ART

shades over imperceptibly into the second condition, that of beauty as an "incentive bonus."

It should be clear from the quoted texts that
Freud neither denied nor overlooked the existence
of what he called formal beauty, as some of his
critics have alleged; nor did he question that it is
a source of pleasure (he called it ". . . the manifest
part of artistic enjoyment"); nor, finally, did he
suggest that this kind of pleasure was itself re-
ducible to instinctual gratification. What he did
claim was rather that the "latent" instinctual
gratification was "far more potent" than the "manifest part of artistic enjoyment."

The latent, or hidden, part and the manifest
part are related to each other somewhat like sadism
and ideal are related in acts of cruelty that are
committed in the name of a religious or secular
ideology. The executioners in the lower echelons
are probably always sadists pure and simple, but
the real ideologist is of a different ilk; for him,
sadism provides the motor force, while the ideal
hides the nature of his activities from him and
makes them respectable; without the latter, he
would not permit himself the torture and the
bloodshed.

In a similar way, the "formal beauty" of, say, a
female nude makes it possible to consummate,
without guilt or shame, the sexual pleasure of the
view (see Fig. 1).

That the quality of beauty does indeed carry the

forbidden gratification along somewhat like corrupt politicians ride into office "on the coattails" of a popular national candidate with spotless reputation, is shown by the many legal proceedings in which the court has to decide whether a particular publication is or is not pornographic. The experts on one side claim that the respective piece is a work of art and that sexual stimulation, if any, is accidental. The experts on the other side claim that the work in question has little or no artistic merit and is merely prurient.

The degree of desexualization necessary for passage varies according to time, place, and circumstances. Where there is none, the product will be classified as a stimulant pure and simple rather than as art. On the other hand, desexualization is *hardly ever complete,* and even in extreme cases there is some remnant of direct gratification. A remark by Sir Kenneth Clark (1956) regarding the nude seems pertinent in this context:

> 'If the nude', says Professor Alexander, 'is so treated that it raises in the spectator ideas or desires appropriate to the material subject, it is false art, and bad morals.' This highminded theory is contrary to experience. In the mixture of memories and sensations aroused by the nudes of Rubens or Renoir are many which are 'appropriate to the material subject'. And since these words by a famous philosopher are often quoted, it is necessary to labour the obvious and say that no nude, however abstract, should fail

[30]

to arouse in the spectator some vestige of erotic feeling, even although it be only the faintest shadow—and if it does not do so, it is bad art and false morals.

The objection to the Freudian theory on the ground that it deals with what is aesthetically irrelevant is sometimes presented in this form: that psychoanalytic interpretations of a work of art, by dealing only with the content and not with the quality of execution, are equally applicable to great art and to trash and so do not come to grips with the problem of "art," i.e., of artifacts of quality. This criticism has been advanced very frequently; the following passage from the 1960 Reith Lectures of Professor Edgar Wind may be quoted as a particularly well-considered expression of it:

Although it is now generally understood that the methods of depth psychology were designed to uncover pre-conceptual types of emotional life, it is not always realized that these types are also pre-artistic. It is no reproach to the psychoanalytic method that, when applied to artistic creation, it tends to wipe out the difference between great art and mawkish art: reduced to the diffuse level of the subliminal, refinements of perception are likely to vanish. On the other hand, if it were clearly stated that it is precisely the infra-artistic kind of impulse that is to be anatomized in psycho-analytic studies, their genuine contribution to artistic psychology might be better defined than it is at present [p. 178].

[31]

The statement is correct, at least as far as the id approach to works of art is concerned, which is indeed the one most often found in the literature,[1] except for two facts not considered by Professor Wind: for one, quality—"formal beauty," in Freud's language—is indeed, as we have seen, part of his theory as a source of, albeit minor, pleasure in itself and as the condition under which the "infra-artistic impulse" can be unleashed; then, if Professor Wind requests that it be "clearly stated that it is precisely an intra-artistic kind of impulse that is to be anatomized in psycho-analytic studies" in order that "their genuine contribution to artistic psychology might be better defined," attention must be called to the fact that Freud has done just this. He stated in a paper on Dostoevsky:

> Four facets may be distinguished in the rich personality of Dostoevsky: the creative artist, the neurotic, the moralist and the sinner. . . . The creative artist is the least doubtful: Dostoevsky's place is not far behind Shakespeare. . . . *Before the problem of the creative artist analysis must, alas, lay down its arms* [1927b, p. 177; italics added].

In his introduction to Marie Bonaparte's study of Edgar Allen Poe, Freud wrote:

> Investigations of this kind are *not intended to explain an author's genius,* but they show what

[1] The writings of Ernst Kris (1952) are a conspicuous exception.

[32]

motive forces aroused it and what material was offered to him by destiny [1933, p. 254; italics added].

This should clarify the point. But psychoanalysis has actually not remained restricted to the study of the "material offered by destiny"; as I have already suggested, it can, in fact, contribute to the understanding of formal beauty and of quality itself by the possibility of a psychoanalytic approach to the beauty of configurations. This will have to be considered again later in another frame of reference.

In the theory under discussion Freud was, of course, speaking of the reaction of the great majority of people; his statement does not exclude that there may be a few—the connoisseurs—for whom this "manifest" artistic pleasure in "formal beauty" is more important than the "latent" content or even, in some cases, the only important thing. In such cases, a *displacement* from content to form has taken place—a process about which more will have to be said later.

(b) Wishes Frustrated by External Objects

There is nothing forbidden in the dream of the little office girl that a handsome young boss may fall in love with her and propose marriage to her. True, the wish is a derivative of the forbidden oedipus fantasy of childhood, and in some cases

[33]

ROBERT WAELDER

this origin may sufficiently color it so that the pro-
hibition which adhered to the oedipus wish may
become attached to the derivative as well. But for
itself alone, it is an acceptable derivative. However, the fantasy is so rarely realized that it seems
childish to entertain it seriously, and an adult has
to be ashamed of it; although she may indulge in
it in a movie house, in the community with hun-
dreds of other spectators, fellows in regression, and
with the excuse of the visual qualities or the quality of the performance of the actors which the film
may offer. A residue of embarrassment may remain, and conversation upon leaving the movie
house may somewhat pointedly be centered around
the merits of the acting or the photography, as
though to indicate that one was not naïvely en-
grossed in the story but had enjoyed it only for
its formal merits.

There is a large class of artifacts which help to
conjure up the real or alleged delights of the past
—of one's own childhood when one was still pro-
tected and unencumbered by responsibilities, or of
a past age that appears happier or nobler than
ours. Representations of rural views often elicit
memories of happy childhood days spent in rural
environs. A painting like that by Francisco Guardi
(Fig. 2) can elicit nostalgic feelings in twentieth-
century men because it may suggest simpler times
in which life, supposedly, was still fulfilled; or, in
the words of the poet Stefan George,

[34]

wo sich leben
zu ende lebt in Welt von Gott und Bild.
[where existence
is ringed by worlds of image and of God].

Those who furnish their homes with period pieces try to build an atmosphere of a past age—be it the simpler life suggested by American colonial; or the vigor, self-confidence, and sobriety of the enterprising burgher suggested by the Dutch seventeenth century; or the elegance suggested by the French Rococo; or the quiet idyllic life suggested by Austrian Biedermeier of the age of Schubert.

These artifacts are tools that facilitate the bitter-sweet sentiment of *nostalgia*. This aspect of art is quite common; the nineteenth-century painter Ludwig Richter said that art is a kind of nostalgia.

Many structures of the past, buildings and places of worship, and especially whole cities or villages that have been preserved or resurrected, have an appeal of this kind. In places where nature and artifacts seem to blend into perfect unity and which have remained fairly unchanged and continuously lived in, giving us an illusion of timelessness—as, for instance, in Conques (Fig. 3)—the impression is particularly strong. We often speak of the "charm" of a place to characterize the surviving past. A painter once talked to me about the walks in Paris which he loved best and took most often, and added: then one can dream.

[35]

Yet hardly anybody who indulges in such dreams would ever actually want to live in the past age, were such option open to him, any more than an adult would actually choose to be a child again. We enjoy, as visitors, the charm of places like those mentioned, but we would not like to live in them in their halcyon days, with all the squalor, the disease and the callousness that would be part of it. We may look at the magnificent Baroque palace which Prince Eugene of Savoy, Co-Commander with Marlborough in the Wars of the Spanish Succession and victor over the Turks, had built for himself in Vienna and experience it as truly "life-enhancing," to use Berenson's favorite expression; it suggests a life of nobility and style. Yet, when we hear of the utterly inhuman treatment of the severely sick in Eugene's army, we shall hardly opt for the age in its entirety. The artistic remains of the great age of Flanders are entrancing; but who would actually wish to live in an age in which a little princess of Burgundy had for her enjoyment a retarded child whom she led around on a leash?

Nostalgia looks back at one aspect of the past and idealizes it while conveniently forgetting the rest. The tourist who has visited these places of beauty by modern conveyances gladly returns to his hotel which offers him twentieth-century conveniences and safety.

*The Question of Aesthetic Relevance and the Aura
of a Work of Art*

It may well be held that the pleasure which
Freud described, while perhaps decisive for the
financial success of a movie, has nothing to do with
its aesthetic qualities proper and is therefore irrelevant for an aesthetic theory. This is, of course, a
matter of semantics; if aesthetics is defined as that
branch of philosophy that deals with the nature of
beauty, the enjoyment of literary content is left
outside. In that case, Freud's theory would have
to be formulated somewhat in the following way:
that there is a conscious and an unconscious *reaction to art,* the former due to its aesthetic qualities, the latter to its more or less hidden literary
content, and that aesthetic merits make it possible
for otherwise inadmissible content to pass.

But the reaction to works of art is not merely a
matter of aesthetics in the narrow sense; a number
of other factors enter into the cluster of sensations.
Associations and fantasies have much to do with it.
Medieval art will appeal more strongly in its original environment—as in the churches for which it
was made—than in a museum; it will also appeal
more strongly in a museum housed in a medieval
structure in a still at least partially medieval
environment, such as the Musée de Cluny, than in
a modern reconstruction of a medieval building
set in a modern metropolis, such as the New York

[37]

Cloisters; and it will appeal more strongly in the latter than in an altogether modern museum building. This we speak of as "atmosphere."

There is also a great difference in our responses to the original and to the most faultless replica, not exempting cases in which not even the trained eye can detect the difference without the benefit of laboratory examination. An original piece of Shaker furniture will appeal much more to us than the technically most perfect modern copy; only the former carries the associations of a simple culture in which man and cosmos were still at one, while the latter carries the rather unpleasant and disillusioning associations of an affluent society for which the form of life of men of the past has become a form of luxury and a source of special excitement. The Marxist poet and critic, Walter Benjamin, spoke of the "aura" of a work of art. In all these instances, we are dealing with *associations* which are an important part of our response to a work of art even though they may not be called "aesthetic" in a narrow sense.

The Development of Taste

Pleasing fantasy activities undergo the same development of growing complexity and sophistication that we encountered in discussing the changing taste in configurations. Just as melodies, rhythms, or color schemes may become uninteresting or appear childish, so may the literary motifs of yesterday appear naïve today. A simple "story," dramatically told, about a child who walked down the road and fell into a ditch may be fully satisfying to a child of two or three; he may request to be told it time and again without the slightest alteration, and each time greet the well-known outcome with delight. The same story is not acceptable on a higher level of sophistication. The simple mishap will have to be replaced by misfortunes which have significance for a later age; the road toward it can no longer be unexplained or direct. Motives will have to be invented and detours will have to be added. Perhaps the hero (or victim) will repeatedly circumvent his obstacle, only to meet new ones thereafter. Tension will be built up and only partially released, to be built up again until eventually a happy ending will put an end to all ordeals. And even this may come to appear trite and the story may end inconclusively, with a question mark, or with the indication of a continuing Odyssey.

The plot in *Romeo and Juliet* would not be possible today; the motif of adolescent lovers whose union is prevented by their families has no tragic appeal to us and would have to be greatly refined to become possible; the final plot of escape, with misunderstandings leading to suicide, is unthinkable, except perhaps as a mockery. Complications due to mistaken identity—as, for instance, between a girl and her identical twin whose existence nobody suspected, a stock in trade in comedy since Menander—are equally unthinkable in the contemporary theater, except perhaps in a play about a play, as a kind of period piece with nostalgic implications.[2] The heart, said Stefan George, is an important organ but it is no longer possible in poetry.[3]

The reversal of taste which is typical of the development in the oral sphere has its analogy in the literary, the visual, and the auditory spheres. Sweetness becomes repellent not only in chocolates but also in landscapes, portraits, or melodies. And the development of taste away from the primitive and, in some cases, its actual reversal may become, in literature, music, or the visual arts, the hallmark of an elite, just as the development of taste from the sweet to the tart is a sign of adulthood and aspired to for that very reason.

In a discussion of a successful modern existentialist play, Diana Trilling (1964) raises the question of how the dismal existentialist message of

[2] This motif still satisfied educated audiences around the turn of this century in a German verse drama by Ludwig Fulda; this shows that it is not only in weapons technology that greater changes have taken place in recent decades than have previously in many centuries.

[3] In discussing the role of boredom in the evolution of new art forms, Ortega y Gasset (1948) remarks: "Cicero still said *latine loqui* for 'speaking Latin'; but in the fifth century Apollinarius Sidonis resorted to *latialiter insusurare*. For too many centuries the same had been said with the same words."

[40]

the absurdity of all life can appeal to large audiences of people whose behavior does not indicate that they look upon their lives and their concerns as absurd; she suggests that interest in a philosophy of this kind may now have become a badge of distinction:

> . . . we have to be rid of an assumption implicit in the sociology of culture, that art necessarily refers to the life to which it is directed. I would propose a quite opposite premise that art today primarily refers not to life at all, not to the external or objective entity with which it is dealing or to which it is appealing, but only to other art. It undertakes to transcend the democratic actuality by means of a series of signals by which each of us establish our moral or spiritual exclusiveness within the common human situation [p. 223].

It is, albeit on a much higher level, the story of the adolescent's cigaret.

3. An Ego Approach:
The Economy of Solutions

Quel maestro si drizza alla perfezione del arte, del quale l'opera e superata dal giudizio.

Perfection in art is achieved by the master whose work is ruled by judgment.

—LEONARDO DA VINCI

Freud's Second Approach to Aesthetics

While the id approach to aesthetic phenomena is widely known (though often misunderstood and misapplied), the existence of an ego approach is far less known, partly, probably, because it came into being before a distinct ego psychology was developed and partly because it appeared in the context not of art but of a psychology of jokes and of the comic in general.[1] According to this theory, the pleasure which we experience in jokes is due

[1] Ernst Kris has called attention to the fact that here we have a genuine aesthetic theory.

to a sudden, unexpected, break-through of sexual or aggressive impulses out of their ordinary confinement, a sudden liberation from the pressures of self-control and a release of inhibitions; i.e., in Freud's words, "to the momentary suspension of the expenditure of energy upon maintaining repression, owing to the attraction exercised by the offer of a bonus of pleasure" (1925, p. 66).

While part of the pleasure still lies in the satisfaction of desires ordinarily banned from expression—sexual impulses, particularly of the anal and phallic stages, or aggressive impulses—it lies also in the surprise and in the form in which this release has unexpectedly occurred, the way in which the censor has been cheated of his prey. Freud concludes:

All three [forms of comic phenomena] are agreed in representing methods of *regaining from mental activity a pleasure* which has in fact been lost through the development of that activity. For the euphoria which we endeavour to reach by these means is nothing other than the mood of a period of life in which we were accustomed to deal with our psychical work in general with a small expenditure of energy—the mood of our childhood, when we were ignorant of the comic, when we were incapable of jokes and when we had no need of humour to make us feel happy in our life [1905b, p. 236; italics added].

The idea of economy may stand us in good stead when we search for the ego aspect of beauty.

[43]

The Ego Aspect of Beauty

The "ego," in the later psychoanalytic model, is a problem-solving agent. *Quality* of performance lies, first, in the fact that a solution has been found when the task had seemed unsolvable, or would have been unsolvable by ordinary human effort; second, in the perfection of a solution; and finally in its elegance, the economy of means. These are the characteristics that make the beauty of a solution and I suggest that they constitute the ego aspect of beauty.[2]

These characteristics can be seen not only in the arts but in our daily activities. We consider it a "beautiful" solution of a problem if everything has been achieved that we had set out to achieve and, in particular, if this has been done with a minimum of effort.

In the year 1937, when once again war clouds were gathering over Europe, President Roosevelt called in a famous speech for the "quarantining of the aggressors." He wanted the United States to take an active part in encouraging resistance to the

[2] The stimulus for this formulation came from Freud's aforementioned theory of the comic; it should be added, however, that while in the case of the joke the saving of expenditure upon inhibition is due, in the main, to a sudden disappearance of inhibition (or, one might say, to the fact that the Maginot Line had been outflanked), beauty, in the above-presented hypotheses, lies in the economy of a solution found by an active ego. However, rudiments of this aspect may be found in the comic as well.

expansionism of Hitler Germany and of Japan, and he tried to win public support for such a policy. But the reaction to the speech showed immediately that the President had gone farther than public opinion was ready to follow; even loyal New Dealers were indignant at what they felt was another attempt at "meddling" in the affairs of Europe. Roosevelt made a strategic retreat—if indeed his speech had ever been more than a trial balloon. In the next Presidential Press Conference, a reporter asked—I do not know whether he acted on his own initiative or had been encouraged to do so—whether the quarantining of aggressors implied the repeal of the mandatory neutrality law, just enacted, that made it obligatory for the United States to keep its ships at home in the event of war abroad and forbade the sale of arms to belligerents. Mr. Roosevelt replied with his famous smile: "No—and that is the beauty of it."

If it had been possible for the United States to organize and to back up a European stop-Hitler front without entering into any commitments, without even permitting the sale of arms to actively resisting nations—if so much could have been achieved without any costs and risks at all—that, indeed, would have been beautiful.

Psychoanalysis is certainly aware of the cruelty which is involved in the passion for bullfights. But these performances are not merely crude sadistic exhibitions like the *munera* in the Roman circus;

[45]

the people admire the beauty in the performance of the great toreador, and it is this quality rather than the mere killing of the bull that makes the fame of the great bullfighter. The people admire his calm and his self-control and the strict economy of his movements. The greatest toreadors have been those who time and again dodge the onrushing bull only in the last split second and with the least movement of the body so that the animal misses them by a mere inch. The bullfight dramatically contrasts the blind strength and uncontrolled fury of the beast with the originally much smaller, but cerebrally controlled and enhanced strength of man. David conquers Goliath, mind triumphs over matter.

The Freudian theory, discussed earlier, of the "incentive bonus" of "formal beauty" can be brought to bear on this situation. There is the secret sadistic excitement and gratification, hidden from oneself or at least from others; there is also the "formal beauty" which makes its expression possible. The beauty seems to lie in the economy of means; a formal quality which, in this case, can itself be seen as satisfying a fantasy, viz., that of the victory of mind over brute force.

Games of chess have often been called beautiful, and special beauty prizes are awarded in some tournaments. One of the most famous games in the history of chess was the so-called immortal game Anderson-Kieseritzky (1851); it was a king's gambit in which White won through a combination involving the sacrifice of a bishop, both rooks, and the queen, and checkmating his opponent with what was left after the massacre. The impression of beauty is conveyed by the demonstration that crude numbers do not count against superior intellect.

So-called chess problems in which one side has to be checkmated in a limited number of moves—usually two or three—appeal to the devotee through their beauty. In this case beauty does not lie in the victory of David over Goliath. The attacker—White—is virtually always greatly superior in force and his victory is a foregone conclusion; in actual life, in a tournament, Black would have thrown in the sponge long ago. But victory, however secured, seems to require many more moves for full consummation than are allowed for by the terms of the problem. The task lies in finding the one move that alone will make the opponent's defeat inevitable in the prescribed number of moves. The beauty of a fine chess problem lies in the fact that a rather inconspicuous move, which at first glance seems to be irrelevant to the issue of the game or even to take the player farther away from the goal of victory, should turn out to be the very one that secures victory in record time. The disproportion between the inconspicuous effort and the decisive result combines with the element of surprise to convey the aesthetic pleasure.

[47]

I remember in my youth a Hungarian soccer player who was hired by a Viennese club. He had been famous for years, but he was now beyond the prime of youth and putting on weight. On the playing field he seemed lazy and hardly ever ran any distance after the ball, to the frequent annoyance of the spectators. But whenever the ball chanced to get into his vicinity—and that happened rather often because he was supremely well placed—there was acute danger for the other team. With rapid but sure appraisal of the situation he played the ball precisely to the best possible point. The beauty of the performance often aroused the enthusiasm of the crowd.

Beauty in Science

Pythagoras discovered that in musical harmony the lengths of the chord stand in simple numerical relationships such as 1:2, 2:3, 3:4. The discovery aroused much enthusiasm; the explanation of the harmony was beautiful in its simplicity. It is no wonder that, as happens so often in the history of human thought, its importance was vastly overrated; the Pythagoreans believed that in whole numbers and their relations they held the key to the understanding of the entire universe.

Scientific theories have often been felt to be beautiful; great scientists have mentioned this sensation as the greatest reward of their efforts and sometimes as the guiding light along the road.

The scientist [said Henri Poincaré (1906)] studies [nature] because he takes pleasure in it, and he takes pleasure in it beause it is beautiful. If nature were not beautiful, it would not be worth knowing and life would not be worth living. I am not speaking, of course, of that beauty that strikes the senses, of the beauty of qualities and appearances. I am far from despising this but it has nothing to do with science. What I mean is that more intimate beauty which comes from the harmonious order of its parts and which a pure intelligence can grasp.

... It is, then, the search for this special beauty, the sense of the harmony of the world, that makes us select the facts best suited to contribute to this harmony; just as the artist selects those features of his sitter which complete the portrait and give it character and life. . . . It is because simplicity and vastness are both beautiful that we seek by preference simple facts and vast facts. . . . Thus, we see that the care for the Beautiful leads us to the same selection as the care for the useful. Similarly, economy of thought, that economy of effort which, according to Mach, is the constant tendency of science is a source of beauty as well as of practical advantage [p. 22].

Some scientists have claimed that beauty is a safe guide in the search for truth. P. A. M. Dirac, for instance, one of the fathers of quantum mechanics, said:

It is true that the ultimate goal of theoretical physics is merely to get a set of rules in agree-

[49]

ment with the experiment. But it has always been found that highly successful rules are highly beautiful and ugly rules are of only restricted use. In consequence physicists generally have come to believe in the need for physical theory to be beautiful, as an overriding law of nature. It is a matter of faith rather than logic.

Dirac mentions as an example Schroedinger's wave mechanics, a beautiful way of deriving the data of quantum theory; it did not, at first, dovetail with the facts and Schroedinger came close to discarding the idea in discouragement. But the incongruity turned out to be merely due to the fact that one aspect of the matter was as yet unknown. Dirac concludes:

> The moral of the story is that one should have faith in a theory that is beautiful. If the theory fails to agree with the experiment, its basic principles may still be correct and the discrepancy may be due merely to some detail that will get cleared up in the future [1954, p. 268f.].

That beautiful rules are often successful ones in theoretical science is due to the fact that those theories are scientifically successful which permit one to see apparently different facts as manifestations of the same principle; but this is also what impresses us as beautiful. Occam's razor—the law of parsimony in abstract concepts—defines something like a *condominium between the realm of truth and the realm of beauty.*

[50]

Examples from the Arts

That there is beauty in precision and brevity is obvious in the short poem, the fable, the epigrammatic statement. Strobaeus tells us that Socrates, asked what happiness was, replied: Pleasure without remorse. In this terse answer—three words in English, two in ancient Greek—there is condensed a whole theory of human life. It would take a while to make this theory explicit, and if this were done, most of the feeling of beauty would be gone.

In such products, very small differences are decisive; as Mark Twain put it: "the difference between the right word and the almost right word is like the difference between lightning and the lightning bug."

These considerations apply equally to the products of the abstract styles in painting and sculpture which are a kind of visual epigram (see Fig. 4). But they also apply to a much wider area, for, as the contemporary sculptor Fritz Wotruba put it, "it has always been, and will always remain, the supreme goal of those who are really working to find ever more simple and more precise forms of expression, in order to become ever more clear and articulate."

A Chinese proverb says that a picture can tell as much as a thousand words. Perhaps we may add that if it can do the job of ten thousand words, it is a great picture.

This is true, first of all, of good illustration. A drawing by a contemporary artist, Andrée Ruellan (Fig. 5), lets us grasp at one glance something of the ironic inevitability of human destiny. The drawing shows a small family group—husband, wife, and child. The young woman is obviously not fulfilled; she is beginning to put on weight. The man shows signs of strain, but he is erect and bearing up bravely. Between them is their little boy, still unaware, probably growing up to repeat the same lot. We get a feeling of the relentless power of Eros through which life is kept going and the individual sacrificed to the species.

The same parsimony can be found outside the anecdotical as well. The anonymous Greek sculptor of a mule, one of the finest pieces of Greek art in the Vatican collections, lets us grasp in very simple forms the essence of this animal as he conceived it—a hybrid, half aggressive, half sly, with one character expressed by the right, the other by the left, side of the head (Figs. 6 and 7).

Velasquez's portrait of Pope Innocent X, in the Palazzo Doria-Pamphili, painted almost exclusively in tones of red, tells us probably as much about the Church at the time of the Counter Reformation as might be learned from a lengthy essay.

One may wonder how many words would have been necessary to express the half-mystical outlook of the aging Rembrandt which one can get at one glance from, for example, his etching of a reclining

Negress whose nude body shades over into the darkness of the background (Fig. 8).

Against this interpretation of the ego aspect of beauty—perfection and economy of means—it may be held that the opposite of Spartan economy, viz., exuberance and delight in ornament, has often been the cause of aesthetic pleasure as, for instance, in flamboyant Gothic and in Baroque. Our hypothesis seems to be based on the appreciation of understatement; but there have been times and cultures that delighted at overstatement.

This is a serious objection, but perhaps not an unanswerable one. The appeal of forms like those of flamboyant Gothic or of Baroque seems to lie partly in the appeal of a *configuration,* a pattern of tension and discharge, and such patterns, as we have seen, can appeal on any level of complexity; and partly it is due to the *content* of a fantasy. The exuberance of Baroque, for instance, conveys a feeling of power and earthly grandeur as is appropriate to the age of the triumphant Counter Reformation and monarchic absolutism. But it does not lie in the perfection and elegance of solutions, i.e., is not "ego" beauty proper. It may, of course, have the latter quality too—*if* the impression is made with fewer lines than would have seemed necessary.

This aspect of beauty is the more appreciated the more eye and judgment are trained. For a minority —the connoisseurs—it may become the major, and occasionally the only, source of enjoyment. We then have a shift, partial or total, from id pleasure to ego pleasure.[3]

The Development of Taste

We noticed in the case of the id aspect of beauty, the satisfaction of fantasy, that there is a process of growing sophistication, from the simple satisfaction of a wish to ever-longer detours. The plain wish fulfillment becomes stale, and more and more obstacles have to be introduced, and tensions built up until they are granted relief—if they are granted it at all. In a similar way, the beauty of scientific theories becomes stale, the satisfaction too complete. Experience shows that nature is not all that simple. The theory of the Pythagoreans, who believed the Universe to be comprehensible in terms of integers, or of the Newtonians, who believed all nature—and, perhaps, society as well— to be comprehensible in terms of laws of attraction similar to Newton's law of gravitation, seem quite naïve to us. New theories emerge which take account of new facts and new complications; they

---

[3] In what we call sublimation we can perhaps distinguish between two types: (a) the displacement of a drive from one subject to another, more acceptable one; and (b) the genuine substitution of ego (or superego) pleasure for instinctual pleasure. The latter case is more than a mere displacement of energies; the whole process is raised to another level. We must look upon it as a stimulation of ego activities by instinctual drives, a process the possibility of which seems to depend on native ability. Any displacement of energies in these cases is contingent upon the possibility of this stimulation.

are also beautiful by reducing the ever-richer canvas of nature to order. But their simplicity is the simplicity of a higher order, as it were; their beauty lies in unity in complexity, i.e., in a kind of rhythm between richness and order, complexity and simplicity.

The present situation in science is described by Charles Coulston Gillispie, a noted historian of science, in these words:

> However congenial Aristotelian physics was to the self-knowledge of the minds that elaborated it, nature is not like that, not an enlargement of common sense arrangements, not an extension of consciousness and human purposes. She is more elusive, *more coquettish* perhaps and infinitely more subtle, hiding her ways from the merely dogged or the worthy, and only occasionally yielding to the truly curious those glimpses of great order and altogether inhuman beauty which are the reward for him who strikes the right note . . . [1960, p. 13].

In the case of science, this development is due, on the whole, to growing experience which makes previous theories obsolete rather than to any boredom and the need for new stimulation—though the latter has a share in letting people look for new facts beyond the known horizons. But in the field of art the same process is entirely a matter of surfeit, boredom, and the need for new stimulation—of the development of taste. The organization of space in a picture may thus develop from simple to more complex arrangements, and from the static to the dynamic, as, for instance, from Giovanni Bellini to Poussin and Rubens. And if at a later stage there is an apparent return to simpler patterns, as there often has been, this return is, except for cases in which a tradition was actually lost or willfully discarded, not a straight resumption of an earlier position; rather, it is conscious archaizing. The geometric simplicity of a Mondrian painting is not the same as that of a Navaho design; its effect is dependent upon the fact that the beholder is familiar with Western art from the fifteenth to the twentieth centuries.[4]

4 See Gombrich (1960).

4. A Superego Approach:
The Transcendence of Nature

> ... *l'art* ... *l'expression la plus haute*
> *de notre secession d'avec du reste de*
> *cosmos—le monument hautain de cet*
> *exile qui nous fait hommes.* . . .
>
> [. . . art . . . the highest expression of
> our secession from the rest of the cos-
> mos, the proud monument of that ex-
> ile that has made us men. . . .]
> —VERCORS

The Theory of Humor

If we can speak of an id aspect and an ego aspect in the impact of art, we may wonder whether there is not a superego aspect, too.

A form of aesthetic pleasure that stems from superego operations was indeed outlined by Freud in his paper on humor. It deals with humor not in the wide sense of the word, which encompasses all comic phenomena including the joke or the cartoon, but only in the narrow sense, in which it refers to the high form of fun which is at once merry and wise and which elicits a mild smile rather than explosive laughter.

> Like jokes and the comic, humour has something liberating about it; but it also has something of grandeur and elevation, which is lacking in the other two ways of obtaining pleasure from intellectual activity [Freud, 1927a, p. 162].
> [Freud places humor, taken in this sense,] among the great series of methods which the human mind has constructed in order to evade the compulsion to suffer—a series which begins with neurosis and culminates in madness and which includes intoxication, self-absorption and ecstasy [p. 163].

I should like to illustrate this method with an example which is similar to the one used by Freud in the quoted paper; like the latter, it is a remark made by a doomed man in one of the last moments of his life. A French aristocrat, at the time of the Terror in the French Revolution, was walking up the stairs to the guillotine; he made a wrong step and almost fell. Turning to the spectators, he said with a smile: "A superstitious Roman would now have turned back." In the age of classicism, every educated person knew of the Roman trait to which he alluded.

The remark pretended that the speaker was still free to turn back if he so wished, but that he refused to do so because he was not given to super-

[58]

stition and would not take the little mishap as a portent of evil things to come. Had he actually believed that this was the case, he would have been psychotic; but he only pretended to believe it, playfully, and so assumed a higher position, above the fate that was about to end irrevocably his physical existence, and refused to succumb mentally to a destiny which he was powerless to avert.

Freud saw the essence of the humorous effect in the fact that the person who "adopts a humorous attitude towards others . . . [behaves] towards them as an adult does towards a child when he recognizes and smiles at the triviality of interests and sufferings which seem so great to it" (p. 163), and he saw in the assumption of this attitude toward oneself—as shown, for instance, by the condemned aristocrat in our anecdote—the original form of the humorous attitude. This attitude thus "consists in the humorist's having *withdrawn the psychical accent from his ego and having transposed it on to his super-ego*" (p. 164; italics added).

The ability to step back and take a look at oneself from an imaginary observation point—the self-consciousness or the transcendence of one's self as it has been called by philosophers, or a platform within the ego *(eine Stufe im Ich)* as it has been called in psychoanalysis—is the essence of the superego function. No sense of humor can develop in organisms in which this transcendence or "platform" is absent, as seems to be the case with animals; or where the cathexis of objects or ideas is so intense that it is not possible to emancipate oneself even temporarily from them in order to assume a detached position toward them as is the case, for instance, with the aggrieved, the fanatic, and the paranoid; one does not jest or trifle with holy things.

Humor is thus one of the cases in which man rises above the situation and *preserves his narcissism intact in the midst of disaster*. In Freud's words:

> The grandeur of it clearly lies in the triumph of narcissism, the victorious assertion of the ego's invulnerability. The ego refuses to be distressed by the provocations of reality, to let itself be compelled to suffer. It insists that it cannot be affected by the traumas of the external world; it shows, in fact, that such traumas are no more than occasions for it to gain pleasure [p. 162].

Other Forms of the Conquest of Fate

This attitude is in some way similar to the one displayed in the lines of Horace which Freud seems to have liked:

Si fractus illabatur orbis,
Impavidum ferient ruinae.

[If the round sky should crack and fall upon him, The wreck will strike him fearless still.]

It is also the sentiment of "Invictus" Henley:

It matters not how straight the gate,
How charged with punishment the scroll;
I am the master of my fate,
I am the captain of my soul.

But the remark of the doomed man, while identical in content with the claim of the poet, seems to me to express the idea more subtly, more credibly, and therefore more appealingly to some tastes at least. Henley's lines are boisterous and rather hard to believe. We feel a kind of grandeur, but there is at the same time a doubt whether the poet can really make good on his words, whether there is not a point beyond which he would break down. It is hard to believe that it really "matters not how straight the gate, how charged with punishment the scroll."

It is illuminating to consider the difference between the two ways of making the same claim. Henley's way does not convey the feeling of humor; it is rather megalomanic, a defiance in the face of destiny, and elevating in this sense like great oratory. There is no hint of a smile at oneself. The comment of the doomed aristocrat, on the other hand, has that very quality. It has the implication, made explicit in Freud's analysis, of looking at one's own misfortunes, including one's own premature death, as though it were really not very important, and of comforting this suffering creature like a good parent would comfort a child with

[61]

whose little tragedies he feels sympathetic, if condescending, concern.

Both Henley's lines and the aristocrat's comments rise above the event of reality into an imaginary superiority; but while the former is all defiance and aggression, with libido only in self-assertion, the latter shows the milder, desexualized love of the parent for the child, internalized into a comforting attitude of the superego toward the ego. At the same time, we can also discover a difference in economy: in Henley's lines it is as if the world issues were moved with colossal effort; in the comment of the man about to die, it is all a hint. The ego aspect of beauty, economy of expression, is on his side.

There is pleasure in the transcendence of reality, in the triumph over destiny, in the ability to keep one's narcissism intact while the ego perishes. It was a majestic expression of this attitude when, according to the tradition, Jan Hus, tied to the stake and seeing an old woman bring more kindle to it, exclaimed: *Sancta simplicitas!* About to die an agonizing death, he still shows a superiority over destiny that is magnificent—albeit uncomfortably close to the delusional—and that permits him to see something admirable and even sacred in the doings of a weak-minded or fanaticized person who is out to add to his martyrdom.[1]

[1] The remark attributed to Hus is clearly a replica of Jesus' saying: Father, forgive them for they know not what they are

Akin to humor is mellowness, the attitude that W. H. Auden ascribed to Shakespeare's Prospero,

>   the power to enchant
> That comes from disillusion.[2]

These attitudes have been expressed most often in the arts of the word, from which the examples of this chapter have been drawn. They are also capable of expression in pictorial art. In the latter case, we are again dealing with *literary content of a work of art,* as in the dreams and illusions discussed in an earlier chapter.

The Spiritualization of Nature

Humor and wisdom of disillusion are but one manifestation of the human ability to rise above space, above time, and, to a degree, above fate. Other manifestations are the fact that man not only suffers but knows that he suffers, not only enjoys his life but knows that he experiences joy,

---

doing. It becomes clear from Hus's behavior at the climax of his life, in particular from the letter he wrote to his parishioners before leaving for Constance, that he had identified himself with Jesus and was inviting Jesus' destiny. It was probably this identification that struck the contemporaries as blasphemous, as had Jesus' claim of being the Messiah in the earlier crisis, and so brought about the same tragic consummation.

2 This line, incidentally, is not only a correct description of the kind of aesthetic pleasure under discussion; it is also a *beautiful* description. It has itself the quality of beauty because of its epigrammatic condensation of complex thought, i.e., the effect of surprise and the economy of means.

and so knows deeper joy and deeper suffering; or the development of moral standards and with them of moral responsibility, a new dimension of the grandeur and misery of human life; this ability is also the source for the development of ideas about transcending realms of Being, Infinity, the Absolute. Just as art has expressed sexual wishes as fulfilled, it has also often expressed these aspirations. It is above all to this aspect of art that Gisela M. A. Richter's definition applies: "Art is a spiritualization of nature." This aspect may belong in the context of this chapter.

In the case of pictorial art, this is again a matter of literary content. But there is little doubt that this content is a potent element in the total cluster of sensations that are evoked, for instance, by the great works of religious art.

Artistic quality, which in the case of sexual wishes is necessary to bribe the censor, is necessary here either to do homage to the lofty ideals expressed, or to prevent them from appearing as bombast and empty rhetoric.

In the visual arts, the spiritualization of nature is brought about in one of two ways: *through the body* or *against the body,* through appearances or by getting away from appearances.[3] Within Western art, the former is the classic-humanistic tradi-

3 See the discussion of the differences between classic Greek and Christian religious art by Charbonneaux (1943, p. 56f.).

tion, the latter the Christian tradition, with Christian humanism forming a kind of middleground.

The two approaches may be exemplified by two illustrations. A superb Buddha of the fifth century shows the ascetic in complete withdrawal from all earthy concerns, raptured by the thought of the Absolute (Fig. 9). The words by Goethe said about the deceased Schiller may fit this picture of a man still living:

Und hinter ihm, in wesenlosem Scheine,
Liegt, was uns alle bändigt, das Gemeine.
[Behind him lies, unreal and without essence,
That meanness that holds all of us in bondage.]

An amphora handle of the classic period shows sexual nature ennobled (Fig. 10). A silen, one of the satyrs of the entourage of Dionysus, is shown playing the syrinx. He has the hoofs and the horse's ears that befit his half-animal nature. He is shown sitting in the most indecent position, and his penis, an elevation in the plane of his body, is the conspicuous center of the lower part of the figure. But on this body sits a head of serenity and nobility. He plays the syrinx; music was conceived by the ancient Greeks as bringing Orphic measure to the orgastic Dionysiac forces. The bronze almost looks as though it were an illustration of the story, told by Socrates in Plato's *Symposium,* of the hierarchy of love, beginning with physical sexual desire and ending with the love for the *kalokagathon,* the idea

[65]

of the Beautiful and Good, i.e., an illustration of sublimation. Actually the object probably antedated the Platonic dialogue by perhaps half a century; the pictorial representation antedated the philosophical formulation.

In this aspect of art, too, there is a *development of taste* with experience, as there is in the aspects previously discussed; the familiar becomes stale, endless repetition leads to boredom, and wide dissemination makes a phrase or device appear cheap.

Part II

*The Situation of the Arts in the
Contemporary World*

The Place of Art in the
Modern World

AMERICANS, said, Alexis de Tocqueville, are "more adept in the arts that make life easy than in those which embellish it." What is said of Americans or "American culture" is usually true of Western civilization in general and only a little more conspicuous in America than elsewhere; the United States, for better or worse, has been one step ahead of Western Europe along the road, traveled by all, of progressive disintegration of tradition and an ever-expanding rational management of all aspects of life. All non-Western civilizations prior to their contact with the West, and European civilization itself before the Age of the Explorers and the so-called Scientific Revolution, have in this respect been comparatively static. They had reached a plateau in their ability to control their environment, and whatever progress there still was in this direction was so slow as to be unnoticeable except over long periods of time. The life of each generation did not appreciably differ from that of their parents and grandparents, except for the impact of irregular events such as famines, epidemics or wars, and people did not expect the life of their children to be any different from theirs. The attention of the best minds was given to *autoplastic* rather than to alloplastic adjustment.[1] Numerable sages and prophets through the ages have taught that happiness can never be safely based on the goods of the "world" and that the only salvation lies in withdrawal from it. Religions and philosophies provided comfort in misfortune and showed ways in which men could steel themselves against suffering. Confucianism, Buddhism, Stoicism, and Epicureanism developed special techniques in this respect; the "Consolations of Philosophy," which Boëtius, the last of the Romans, as he has been called, wrote in prison while awaiting his execution, is a noble document of this orientation.

These ages also gave much attention to "embellishing" life, which they took as essentially unchangeable. One may wonder whether the people did not progress toward a more effective control of their environment because their best minds were absorbed with the tasks of autoplastic adjustment, or whether this direction of their mind was due to the fact that any attempts at bringing about a sub-

[1] I am following Ferenczi's distinction (1919) between autoplastic and alloplastic adjustment, the former through changing oneself, the latter through changing the environment.

stantial change in the external conditions of life seemed so hopeless an endeavor. It was probably a vicious circle.

In Western civilization, on the other hand, the outlook is *alloplastic,* toward adjusting the environment to human wishes rather than toward adjusting man to his environment. Any kind of frustrated desire, including the frustration of a desire only just awakened, is for moderns merely a challenge to their inventiveness to find a way of satisfying it. Initiative and efficiency are the virtues of modern civilization, while ripeness and wisdom were the most highly prized qualities of autoplastic ages.

In a great masterpiece of late medieval art, the Altar of Issenheim, the decaying flesh of the crucified Christ is depicted with such merciless realism that it comes dangerously close to the limits of the artistically bearable. This feature can be seen in the light of the cruelty of the age and in the light of trends in late Gothic art, particularly in the Germanic orbit. But the place for which the work was destined must also, and perhaps foremost, be considered. The Altar was commissioned by the monastery of St. Anthony in Issenheim. The monastery served as a hospital for the most severe diseases— in that age people did not have the means of providing for any but the gravest afflictions. Most of the patients suffered from leprosy, erysipilas ("St. Anthony's fire"), and syphilis, which at that time

[71]

appeared in virulent form. These wretched suffer-
ers could see the putrified flesh of the Savior on
Golgatha and then the ecstatic glory, in a dazzling
symphony of colors, of the Resurrection. Perhaps
they found some consolation and hope in it.
Viewed against this background, the lurid character of the Crucifixion in the Grünewald Altar appears as *functional in an autoplastic context.*

Our way of doing things is entirely different. We
do not offer patients much in the way of religious
hopes and we would not think of calling on great
masters of the arts to produce artistic illusions. But
we lay the greatest emphasis on the development,
through systematic research, of effective methods
of treatment and prevention. In modern civilization the curse of the aforementioned diseases is
marginal: syphilis has become largely curable, erysipilas is usually brought under control; and although medicine has not yet found a way of curing
leprosy, it has already made it possible to treat
many patients on an ambulatory basis and it is not
fantastic to expect that the disease will be brought
under complete control in the not too distant
future.

Across the street from the Baptistery in Florence
is the little Loggia del Bigallo. It was a place where
women—primarily, presumably, unmarried moth-
ers—dropped their unwanted babies, in the hope
that charitable souls will pick them up and rear
them. The little building is adorned with frescoes

[72]

and sculptures. Again our ways are different. We handle the same problem in child-placing agencies where trained social workers prepare for the adoption of unwelcome children by suitable foster parents, and stand ready to assist the expectant mother with necessary arrangements. But our agencies do not have offices with elaborate ornamentation.

When we compare the sixteenth-century hospital, devoid of any helpful medications but in possession of the glorious Grünewald Altar, with the unadorned modern hospital which has increasingly effective means of controlling illnesses, or compare the Loggia del Bigallo with a modern child-placement agency, we can measure the full difference between an autoplastic, aesthetic civilization and an alloplastic one whose orientation is ethical and utilitarian. It was in view of similar considerations that many men have predicted the decline of the arts with the progress of science and technology. "As civilization advances, poetry almost necessarily declines," wrote Thomas Babington Macaulay in 1825.

In any case, the arts do not fulfill a vital role and do not occupy a central place in modern civilization. The climate is unfavorable for the development of great art. Most important, perhaps, is the fact that under modern conditions few of the most gifted and most ambitious youths will choose art for a career. In many periods of the past, e.g., in the Renaissance, art was a most attractive career;

[73]

it offered to gifted commoners an excellent chance of economic security, status, and even wealth. Today youths with similar endowment have an enormous choice of promising careers: the sciences, engineering, banking, industry, medicine, politics.[2] The story of the conflict between a youth bent on a life devoted to art and a prosaic father forcing him into another, more "practical" career—a story frequent in the nineteenth century in both life and fiction—reflects conditions of a transitional period in which the arts were slowly moving from the center of the scene to the periphery. Today, when the process has already gone very far, few youths have similar unorthodox aspirations.

Thus, in many periods of the past art had the greatest creative talents of the age among its practitioners; there is little likelihood that the same will happen in our time.[3]

[2] In a letter to the Editor of the New York *Herald Tribune* (May 14, 1964) the physicist T. R. Bashow registered his protest against an article, published in that newspaper, in which the absence of outstanding works in fiction, drama, and music was deplored; the letter writer pointed out that in our time beauty can be found in science, and then stated: "Creative minds are no longer interested in becoming the type of artist whose work you can understand. Why make daubs on canvas or spread words on paper when you can change the very environment about you? The earth, and ultimately the universe itself, is our marble block to shape as we can." These words are a characteristic, albeit exaggerated, reflection of the temper of the time.

[3] Implied in this is the assumption that creative talent, as a rule, is in the beginning more plastic and less specialized than is often assumed. The fact that so many Renaissance men were productive in more fields than one—perhaps as painters, sculp-

From this twilight of the arts, architecture is conspicuously exempt. It is very much alive, more so, perhaps, than it has been since the great days of the Baroque. But it is an architecture which has renounced all embellishment and has concentrated on the functional (in an alloplastic sense). It seeks its beauty mainly in qualities of the material, in proportions, and in the perfection of its solutions of utilitarian tasks. In addition to this, part of its

---

tors, goldsmiths, architects, and engineers—seems to support this contention.

It is challenging to contrast two very great men who belonged to different cultures, Goethe and Jefferson. Both were almost exact contemporaries and about equally long-lived, beyond the Biblical life span; both were universal men, active and productive in many fields; each was perhaps the greatest man in his nation's history. Jefferson was politician, statesman, founder of a university, political theorist and writer, architect and inventor; his center was in the *practical*. Goethe's center was in the *contemplative,* as poet, writer, art critic, and perhaps as a naturalist. He is also most impressive for the richness of his personality and his wisdom. His excursions into the practical, on the other hand, were either outright failures, like his attempts at experimental science, or undistinguished, like his service as minister to a princeling.

It is tempting to speculate that this difference may have something to do with the cultural climates in which each man developed: on the one hand, eighteenth-century North America, with enormous opportunities in the political sphere, a wide appreciation of everything utilitarian, and a Puritan distrust of contemplation, which implied leisure, the breeding ground of sin; on the other hand, eighteenth-century Germany, offering little chance for a creative role in the political sphere and no prestige to technicians, but a ranking national position to a great philosopher, poet or playright. Such differences in reward and punishment are likely to encourage individuals with different endowments, and they may even guide the same kind of individual along different roads of development.

[75]

appeal consists in the frankness of its self-represen-
tation, its pride in modesty; in unadorned structures of stark simplicity like the George Washing-
ton Bridge, the man of a technical age seems to say
that this and nothing else is his way of life and that
he does not pretend to be any different from what
he is. One of the earliest pioneers of modern architecture, Adolf Loos, looked upon Victorian and Ed-
wardian decoration as a lie, hence as a moral defect.

The decline of interest has hit the various arts in
different degrees. Owing perhaps to movie and tele-
vision, the dramatic arts have fared better than
poetry and the novel, but, outside the Communist
world, even they have hardly held their own. In
spite of the ease of mechanical distribution, the
stage arts do not seem to command anything like
the interest they held around the turn of the century when the plays of Ibsen and Strindberg,
Hauptmann, Echegaray and Wedekind, and Wag-
ner's musical drama deeply stirred the educated
strata of Europe. The film as major art form of the
mid-twentieth century is perhaps still more a prom-
ise than an accomplished fact.

Things seem to be different in the Soviet Union
and the so-called popular democracies of Eastern
Europe; drama and poetry seem to play a great role
there and to command wide interest. They seem to
serve as escapes from both a drab reality and an
enforced conformity. Oppositional sentiment
which could not be expressed directly in terms of

political and social criticism can find expression in works of art; some films produced in Eastern Europe, for instance, give a rather dismal picture of the moral climate. In such cases, the heretical thoughts take cover partly behind the ambiguity of the artistic statement which is liable to more than one interpretation, and partly behind the artistic merits of the product, the latter analogous to what Freud described in the case of matters forbidden for other reasons. Moreover, art seems to enjoy something of the court jester's license of another age. The authorities probably consider these productions, within limits, as harmless or perhaps necessary outlets for dissatisfactions which could otherwise rise to dangerous heights.

The Function of Painting

Among the arts, painting has probably been hit the hardest by the modern developments. Though more people are visiting art exhibitions and buying paintings today than ever before, the role of painting in the modern world is not clear and its place is not secure.

At first, painting was probably a matter of magic and, in this sense, functional. It is generally assumed that the representations of animals in prehistoric cave drawings had some magical function, presumably connected with hunting.

In a later time, such beliefs faded out, but there

was still magic in painting, in a different sense. People admired the life-likeness of painting, the exact imitation of nature; this quality still has great appeal for the unsophisticated. But what now survives in the wonderment of the naïve gallery goer whom an attendant invited to traverse the room from one end to the other and to notice how the eyes of the portrayed person seem to follow him where he goes—admiration for the life-likeness of the painting—was once a major factor of art appreciation. There are stories which Ernst Kris and Otto Kurz (1934) have shown to be universal, like that of Appelles whose paintings were so lifelike that the birds were said to have picked at the painted crumbs.

The pleasure that was felt at such performances was delight at the fact that man can make a product that rivals nature, i.e., the fantasy of *man the creator*.[4] The men of our age rejoice as much as the ancients at the power of man, but they have far greater achievements from which to derive such satisfactions. They may find a feeling of unlimited power in the solving of the riddles of the atom or the unleashing of its energies, in the deciphering

4 As late as the twelfth century, Hildebert, Bishop of Le Mans, writes with reference to the statues of Rome: "Man gave this town such greatness that the Gods failed to destroy it. These gods admire their own beauty there and would wish to resemble their own statues. Nature could never create gods as beautiful as the admirable images which man has been able to make of them. From these, the gods have taken their features, and it is not their own divinity that men venerate, but the genius of artists."

[78]

of the genetic code or travel into outer space; in comparison with achievements such as these, the power of *trompe l'oeil* art has faded into insignificance. The guilt feelings which, as Kris and Kurz have shown, once adhered to the imitation of nature in art, adhere now to the modern technological achievements.

Painting has also been a means of communication. In the struggle with the iconoclasts, the Churchmen emphasized the need of pictorial representation to familiarize the vast illiterate masses with the Bible story. It was the task of the Christian artist to tell this story time and again and to tell it impressively and movingly.

This function has largely fallen away. There is universal literacy in civilized countries or soon will be, and what visual aids are necessary to illustrate a story can probably be more effectively supplied by photography and moving pictures.

But when increasing literacy made painting more and more dispensable as a means of telling the Gospel story, painting still retained the function of making visual records of persons and events for posterity. If one wished a parent's likeness to be available for oneself and preserved for coming generations, a painting was required. Painting could keep a visual record of important events as well as of humble scenes, of landscapes in various atmospheric conditions, of any kind of objects that seemed worth recording either for what they were

[79]

or for some quality of appearance, or perhaps merely because they could be subject of a pleasing arrangement of shapes, color, and light.

This function of painting has also been largely taken over by photography and cinematography. The countenance of a parent can be permanently preserved by a good photograph, or a good movie, with as much satisfaction for children and grandchildren as would be conveyed by a painted portrait; so can other objects previously recorded in painting for whatever reason. Painting, to be sure, has always tried to combine the recording, illustrative function with a decorative one. Bernard Berenson defined painting as an illustration in terms of a decoration, but this, too, can be done by the camera; there are artistic photographs and movies. There is little need of painting for the purpose of a visual record of reality.

It may be held that the human brain still holds the edge over the machine. Thomas Eakins once needed a picture of his office and sat down to make a drawing of it; somebody suggested that he should not lose his time on it but have a photograph made. Eakins replied that one could not trust a photo.

It is true, as this answer implies, that a photo can give a vastly distorted impression of reality; but so can a drawing or a painting. The borderline between truth and falsehood does not coincide with the borderline between drawing by hand and drawing by light; one can lie with both the hand

[80]

and the camera. The brain is no doubt still vastly superior to man-made machines, but the brain is not excluded from the work of the photographer.

Thus, it seems that the magical function of painting has dropped out because we no longer believe that images influence reality; the sense of triumph at the power of man has found more stunning achievements to feed on; the function of communication in general has been taken over by the printed word and the machine-produced and machine-multiplied picture, still or moving.

Moreover, photography has become a threat to painting not only because it can do so much that heretofore could be done only by the human hand but also, and perhaps above all, for another reason. The enormous distribution of photographs and their mechanical reproductions in postcards, newspapers, magazines have made these views and textures appear cheap or stale; pictures that resemble common photographs have therefore a vulgar or trivial appearance, which they did not have before the photographic age when the eye was not yet conditioned and tired out by endless repetition of certain motifs.

Artists have tried to find a niche for painting under these new circumstances. Paintings were left in a more or less unfinished state. The gradual blending of colors into each other was eliminated. The skeleton of the painter's handiwork such as brushstrokes, which hitherto had to be covered up

[81]

once the work was finished, were permitted to remain visible to the unarmed eye, or even deliberately accentuated. The impressionists piled patches of pure color on the canvas rather than mixing them to the desired shade on the palette, and so left it to the eye of the beholder to blend them. Impressionist canvasses have therefore kept a freshness of vision which academic paintings of the same time whose appearances have been trivialized by endless multiplication are lacking. The freshness, of course, is lost once we have seen a great many impressionist canvasses.

In addition to these devices, artists turned to nonrealistic styles; they looked for inspiration to the preclassical, archaic styles or to a postclassical mannerism. The camera, of course, could not follow them there.

But all this was still makeshift rather than a real solution for the predicament in which painting found itself in the modern age; more radical steps seemed to be necessary to find a place for it under the general conditions of an alloplastic civilization which devalues all art and the special conditions of mechanical image-making which threatens painting in particular. In the last century or so, painting has been an *ancient skill in search of a function* in modern society.

Essentially three solutions for this larger problem have so far been devised:

1. Appearances have been *distorted,* perhaps

for the sake of a stronger expression of emotions, or in order to depict an unconscious world.

2. The illustrative, representational aspect of painting has been largely or even entirely discarded and attention has been concentrated mainly or exclusively on the *decorative* aspect.

3. Painting has been used *reflectively,* in order to play wittily with the art forms of the past.

1. Expressionism and Surrealism

Art, according to this school of thought, has not to represent visible realities but to express an inner life. In expressionism the artist tries to achieve this through distortion of appearances. In surrealism he tries to do so by making a realistic visual recording of dreams and fantasies. Expressionism and surrealism are one in their intention, which is the expression of subjective states of mind without regard to objective, i.e., intersubjective, realities; they differ in respect to their method. In either way, a safe refuge for the visual arts in the age of the camera seems to have been found.

Expressionism may be fortified by a new theory of art and the artist which emerged around the turn of the century. According to this theory, the artist is particularly close to his Unconscious; the Unconscious manifests itself in his works without the artist himself necessarily knowing or ever fully comprehending what he is doing. The production of a

[83]

work of art is thus comparable to automatic writing or sleepwalking. These products of the Unconscious are said to speak directly to the Unconscious of the spectator. It is a conversation from one Unconscious to another. This theory would indeed reserve an unconquerable redoubt for the arts in an age of rationalism.

But the theory is hardly tenable. It is true that the motifs of the work of art often come from the Unconscious. But this feature is not limited to artistic activities; many things that we do, and certainly all imaginative and creative activities, have at least some roots in the Unconscious.

This is true even of the most realistic pursuits, viz., scientific research. Mediocre scientists may correspond, more or less, to the popular image of the scientist as a laborious student who pursues his investigations without any preconceived ideas—a sensitive film, as it were, upon which reality writes its story. But what we know of the life of the great scientists, and what little experience analysts have actually had with creative scientists—experience which, for obvious reasons, cannot be communicated—suggests a different story; the great scientist appears rather as a person who is obsessed by one idea or a few ideas, rooted partly in unconscious fantasies, and who searches in the world for objects which correspond to them. Of course, if he is to be a successful scientist, the flight of his imagination must be sternly controlled by a very exacting reality testing. But this requirement is not exclusive to scientific pursuits; the imagination of the artist also has to be controlled by the ego, albeit with different and perhaps somewhat less exacting criteria, if his products are to have artistic value. Free associations or verbal ejaculations do not, as a rule, rank very high as artistic creations (or, at least, have not done so until very recently).

Thus, there does not seem to be any *fundamental* difference between the arts and other creative pursuits in the relative role of the Unconscious that provides the motifs and of the ego that integrates them into reality.

There is no *prima facie* reason why the Unconscious should necessarily have more of a hand in it when Pierre de Montreux designed the Sainte Chapelle or Velasquez painted The Weavers—both masterpieces of the first rank—than when Charles Darwin pursued throughout his life the idea of evolution through natural selection.[5]

Moreover, the Unconscious out of which the work of art is supposed to rise according to the modern expressionist theory is hardly the Uncon-

5 I do not imply any knowledge of, or hypothesis about, the kind of unconscious fantasy that could have encouraged the rise of such ideas. But it seems unlikely to me, on the basis of general psychoanalytic experience, that the early dedication to, or the lifelong pursuit of, a single idea should be due only to a realistic assessment of its scientific potentialities, and more likely that it has been reinforced from unconscious, emotional sources. Without the latter, it seems unlikely that one would carry on through the inevitable disappointments and rebuffs.

[85]

scious of Freud which consists, in the main, of sediments of individual life; it is rather the Unconscious of Jung, an archaic world common to all of us, or to all people of a race, a nation, or a civilization—a realm through which man is supposed to communicate with the species, the Cosmos, and the Absolute.

In addition to these basic considerations, the expressionist theory seems also open to objection on the ground that not all works of art, or even of great art, need have their roots in the Unconscious; a great portrait, for instance, could be the product of exact observation and mastery of execution combined with a high decorative sense.

2. Art as Mere Decoration

Another approach tries to emancipate art largely or entirely from the illustrative function in which the camera is competing, and to limit it to the decorative. The protagonist of this school was Henri Matisse, a painter of extraordinary decorative inventiveness. While Matisse still composed his decorative patterns around a skeleton of real objects, others have done away entirely with every vestige of real objects; this is the way of nonrepresentational art.

Decorations have been made from the most ancient times of which we have any knowledge. Pottery and textiles, for instance, were made with a view to their being decorative. When objects were depicted, concern for the decorative often went hand in hand with it, in any case in those objects which contemporaries seemed most to appreciate. There have been works of representational art whose decorative qualities have rarely been equaled and never been surpassed, as is the case with the finest examples of Attic black figure painting, medieval illuminations, Sienese and Florentine *trecento* and *quattrocento* painting or Persian miniatures.

But except where the taboo of graven images restricted the freedom of the artificer, it was always felt that art which carries a message in addition to being decorative was art of a higher order than one which is only decorative. I cannot see any reason why this assessment should be revised today. The fact that mechanical picture-making is challenging painting in the area of communication provides a *motive* for looking toward other fields of activity but does not automatically elevate the importance of those other fields.

Besides, decoration may turn out not to be the safe refuge from the hot pursuit of technology after all. Decorations of considerable merit may well soon be made by mechanical means. Already, the microphotography of crystallization processes by Manfred Kage and Hein Gravenhorst has produced works that come close to the appeal of the works of abstractionism and abstract expressionism (Fig. 11).

[87]

3. Historizing Art, or Art about Art

A third function of painting has been practiced by Pablo Picasso: painting as a way of *making pictorial comments on the arts of the past.* Joaquin Mir who had known Picasso in his early youth once said of him that "he does not see anything according to nature but only through the representation in the artifacts made by other artists." From the beginning of his career Picasso has delighted in adapting past art forms to contemporary tasks and mixing apparently disparate styles. Michael Ayrton once analyzed these various combinations. The effects achieved are often striking and always interesting. In an early period, for instance, Picasso produced a surprising blend of the merciless realism of Toulouse-Lautrec with the gracious Rococo of Watteau. His cubist works combined the style of Cézanne, in which a painting is composed of small monochromatic rectangles, and the structure of primitive sculpture, in which figures are reduced to a few simple geometric elements—a combination of a very primitive and a very sophisticated style. The Guernica murals tried to combine the forms of primitive sculpture with Matthias Grünewald's cruel realism in depicting the agony of the Crucified. In their most successful manifestations, these combinations are as surprising and pleasing to the connoisseur of art as are, on a less elevated

level and to another kind of connoisseur, the blending of incongruous tastes in a sauce or a cocktail.

But this kind of thing is of limited appeal; only
those who are thoroughly familiar with the art of
various ages and cultures and whose interest in art
is reflective rather than naïve can enjoy it. This art
is for a small circle only and it has no message for
the masses.

The Gulf between the Initiated and the Masses

The present situation manifests itself sharply in
a more complete separation between the initiated
—the connoisseurs—and the masses than has probably ever existed before. Art that appeals to the
initiated is un-understandable to the masses or
seems risible to them. It is noteworthy that men as
far apart in their philosophies and their tempera-
ments as Adolf Hitler, Harry S. Truman, and N. S.
Khrushchev have expressed themselves on modern
Western art in virtually identical terms. On the
other hand, products that please the masses are
held in contempt by the initiates.

In some degree, a split between those who look
upon content and those who look upon execution,
and between those with naïve tastes regarding content and execution and those with sophisticated
ones, is unavoidable. Yet in the past, the gulf was
not so great that artists could not reach both audiences at the same time by offering something to

[89]

each. It was a festive day for the people of Siena when Duccio's Altar was carried from his studio to its destination in the Cathedral. The people of Florence participated eagerly in the competition for the North Door of the Baptistery, for which the competitors had to submit a sample panel; we can still see the entries of Lorenzo Ghiberti and Filippo Brunelleschi and can sense the level of artistic judgment of the people at the time.

But today, such bridges seem to be broken altogether. Patches of pigment on canvas or, for that matter, on an odd piece of cloth or of furniture are praised as revelations by some and looked upon as meaningless as a dirty palette by others, who see in the enthusiasm of admirers a clear case of the emperor's new clothes.

The Situation in the Plastic Arts

It is somewhat different in sculpture. Magic was once the function of sculpture as it was that of painting; the likeness of a king or a noble that the Egyptians placed in his tomb was probably meant to be a kind of container in which the soul—or that part of the soul that might survive the death of the body—could take rest. This function has gone; most of us do not believe in an immortal soul at all and those who do conceive of it in purely spiritual terms, not in need of any corporeal support.

[90]

The other function of painting, representation and communication, has not been a function of sculpture in anything like the same degree as it was of painting; perhaps, Greco-Roman portrait sculpture comes closest to having been meant as a representation of a likeness.

It is perhaps due to the characteristics of the more durable materials of sculpture—stone and bronze—that the sculptor has usually not aimed at making a deceptively true likeness of his subject— which has usually been man and animal—but rather at *catching something like its essence,* the eternal core, as it were, for perpetuity. The Egyptians expressed it directly; only a part of the soul—the *ka* —was potentially immortal, and the sculptured head was to be the seat of this immortal essence. A realistic portrait was therefore not intended (with some exceptions, particularly in the Amarna period and in the late epochs). It was the *essence* of a person, so to say, which the sculptor tried to preserve for eternity rather than his ephemeral characteristics. The statue was therefore more often a generalized than an individualized portrait, and a king could appropriate the statue of a former ruler by having the name of the latter scratched out and his name substituted for it.

The metaphysical and theological concepts have faded away, but the main stream of sculpture has followed this line, even though with a different philosophy. Guided by the potentialities and the limitations of the material, it has been abstract and monumental rather than realistic or naturalistic, more interested in abstracting essences than in preserving the infinite detail of appearances. Sculpture has therefore been less affected by the competition of modern technology than painting; to see the essence of a human head, or a human figure, or an animal, and to set it down in simple, understandable geometric forms is still a task for the eye and the hand guided by the human brain; photography and cinematography, including the three-dimensional variety, offer no help and threaten no competition. It is perhaps for this reason that modern sculpture seems—to some observers at least—more alive and less esoteric and sectarian than modern painting.

It may also be for this reason that the cleavage between expert taste and mass taste is less wide in sculpture than in painting. There are works in the plastic arts of the last decades that can be appreciated by expert and common man alike as, for instance, many works by Aristide Maillol, John B. Flanagan, Marino Marini, Fritz Wotruba, or Giacomo Manzù.

Painting in the Soviet Union

These problems of Western painting are alien to Soviet art, at least as far as official art is concerned. There is no doubt among the official ideologists in the Communist world about what the proper function of art in this historical period is: it is to *build morale* for the "construction of socialism" and the "construction of Communism." Art should give the people a feeling of pride in their past achievements, of confidence in the way along which they are being led, and of courage and enthusiasm for the task ahead.

There is nothing new in the idea that art should inspire certain feelings. Christian art was supposed to stimulate sentiments of fear and hope, of awe and devotion, and some of the greatest art of all time has been created for purposes of propaganda. Art has also quite specifically been used as a morale builder; Rouget de l'Isle did just that when he wrote the Marseillaise.

There is therefore no *a priori* reason why great art could not be created for the purposes prescribed by Communism. Works of art of considerable quality have in fact been produced in Mexico by painters who were inspired by the ideas of revolutionary socialism, such as Diego Rivera and José Clemente Orozco. But it does not seem to have happened in the Soviet Union; what we know of Soviet painting suggests something similar to Western academic painting in the nineteenth century, with the difference that idealized images of Communist leaders are substituted for idealized images of the leaders of the Victorian age—say, Lenin for Bismarck— and that happy workers and collective farmers, con-

[93]

spicuously conscious of fulfilling a historical destiny, have been substituted for the characters of nine-teenth-century genre painting. These works have not received much applause, even among ideological sympathizers, outside the borders of the Soviet Union; and artists within the Communist orbit show signs of restlessness. Why, one must ask, has the Russian Revolution, which has aroused so much enthusiasm, not given rise to the production of great, or at least of good, art? That it has not is all the more remarkable in view of the fact that at the time of the Revolution Russian artists were in the forefront of the international art world.

The answer must probably be sought in the fact that Soviet art is required to be at once *morale-building and realistic,* i.e., that it is committed to the program of *socialist realism.*

It is not necessarily impossible for art to be both inspirational and realistic; but it can be both only *where the external reality is apt to arouse enthusiasm without much editing.* This happened, for instance, in the halcyon days of nineteenth-century liberalism.

Thomas Eakins's Gross Clinic, painted in 1875 (Fig. 12), showed a medical auditorium. In the fore-ground one sees part of a human body on an oper-ating table, and a few young men are occupied with the patient. Behind them stands the professor of surgery, Dr. Samuel Gross, dominating the pic-ture; in the background are the medical students.

[94]

Dr. Gross's head is placed in the middle of the picture; it is a magnificent head, radiant with intelligence and wisdom. Here, one feels, a better future is being prepared for mankind. The picture was painted at a time when hopes for the infinite progress of mankind, both in the control of its environment and in a moral sense, were at their height, as yet not sicklied over with the pale cast of thought. World wars and mass liquidations had not yet put a question mark to the belief in continuous moral ascendency, and nuclear bombs had not yet dramatized the other side of the coin of applied science. Under these conditions, a painting could be at once inspiring and realistic, with little idealization.[6]

Times have changed since then. Although medicine has more than kept the promises which it then held out, the milk has become just a little sour. We are more aware of complexities, less sure of what we are doing; some of us have come to suspect a utopian element in what René Dubos called "the dreams of reason." Perhaps the sentiment evoked by the painting may even seem a trifle naïve to us. For us, the Gross Clinic, which on account of the

6 Eakins's head of Dr. Gross—or, for that matter, his head of Walt Whitman—is, in fact, idealized, but we hardly notice it and in any case it does not disturb us because we are apt to share the idealizing view. The idealization in Victorian portraiture, on the other hand, is very noticeable to us, and objectionable, because we do not share the implicit values. If there should ever be a time that takes a less elevated view of scientists, it will probably react to the head of Dr. Gross as we react to John Singer Sargeant's duchesses.

[95]

realism of the surgical scene was far in advance of its age, is already a period piece; we may feel a longing for the simple confidence of an earlier age that was so sure of the road it was taking. With us, the painting may kindle a kind of nostalgia.

But let us come back to the question of socialist realism. The socialist reality has not lived up to the promises that Marxism has held out. True, living conditions have improved, after long years of passing through a dark tunnel, but they have improved more slowly than conditions in "capitalist" countries at the same time. The state has not withered away; rather, its hand lies heavier on the lives of the people than before. Migratory pressure, the unmistakable indicator of differentials in living conditions, is westward, not eastward; in every large group of tourists who are allowed to travel to the West, there are likely to be some who use the opportunity not to return.

Some years ago, a joke was told in Hungary about a man who came to a general hospital and asked to be shown the way to the eye-and-ear clinic. He was advised that there was no such department; there was a clinic for diseases of the eye, and a clinic for diseases of the ear, and their respective location was pointed out to him. But the man insisted on being seen by a doctor equally abreast of both. Why? Because, said the man, I don't see what I hear and I don't hear what I see.

Under such conditions, how can art stimulate

[96]

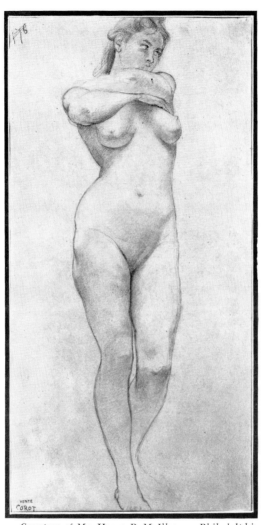

1. CAMILLE COROT: STANDING NUDE

Fundaçao Calouste Gulbenkian, Oeiras, Portugal

2. FRANCISCO GUARDI: VIEW OF MIRA ON THE BRENTA

Photograph by Martin Hürlimann

3. VIEW OF CONQUES (AVEYRON)

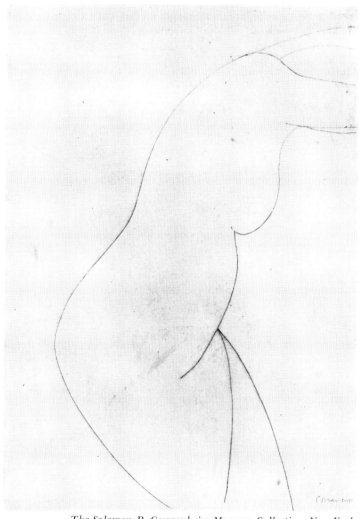

The Solomon R. Guggenheim Museum Collection, New York

4. CONSTANTIN BRANCUSI: NUDE

Private Collection

5. ANDRÉE RUELLAN: FAMILY GROUP

6. HEAD OF A MULE, GREEK, 5TH CENTURY B.C.

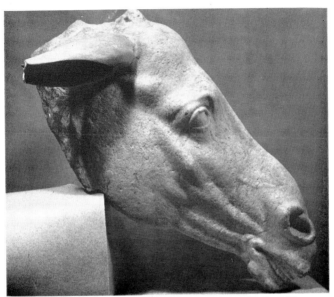

7. HEAD OF A MULE, GREEK, 5TH CENTURY B.C.

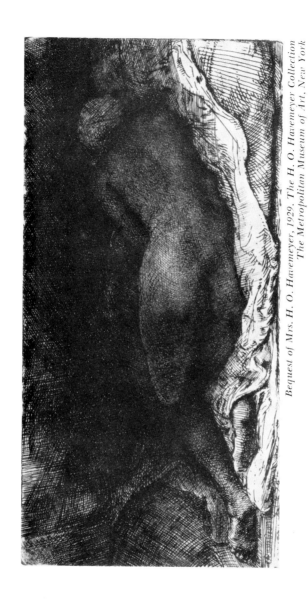

8. REMBRANDT: NEGRESS LYING DOWN

9. STATUE OF BUDDHA, 5TH CENTURY A.D.

10. HANDLE OF AN ETRUSCAN AMPHORA

11. Manfred Kage: Microphotography of crystals

12. Thomas Eakins: The Gross Clinic

enthusiasm and be realistic at the same time? The
former could perhaps be achieved in the way Christian artists treated their subject after the Second
Coming had been indefinitely postponed; they produced highly abstract images to suggest the Divine,
images utterly remote from any observable reality,
like the jeweled mosaics placed in the dimly lit
interior of Byzantine churches or the stained glass
windows of the Gothic cathedrals that filled the
room with a kind of supernatural light. They appealed to the imagination. The Mexican muralists
have done something of the kind in the service of
revolutionary ideas, not without success. But realistic images will not only be largely ineffective for
the purpose in question; they may even, unwill-
ingly, debunk the whole message and make it
appear phoney.

The Philosophical Roots of Socialist Realism

The program of socialist realism is not just a
whim of some Communist rulers, due, perhaps,
to their Victorian tastes. Rather, the combination
of moralistic and realistic elements is deeply rooted
in the structure of Marxist thought and is of its
very essence; for Marxism is a *blend of messianic
prophesy and (presumably) scientific theory*.

In all history known to us, the purposes of men
have at least partially conflicted with those of other
men so that the aims of some could be realized

[97]

only at the expense of those of others. The world has therefore been full of strife; man has often been ruthless in the pursuit of his goals and has not hesitated to use others as means for his ends, with little or no concern for their interests. These conditions have in the past been seen as rooted in the nature of man or the nature of society and therefore either unchangeable or subject to change only to a limited degree, through the acquisition of moral inhibitions, through law, and through institutions which set obstacles to the ambitions of men and help to divert them into less dangerous channels.

But sometime in the eighteenth century the idea emerged that selfishness and strife have no root in human nature and are merely the consequence of an alterable institution, viz., that of private property. Once private property will be abolished, so the idea goes, selfishness and greed, willfulness and strife will be gone, too. As Marx was to formulate it later: "The free development of each is the condition of the free development of all."

Men will then no longer be motivated by concern for themselves, their families or any narrow group with which they are identified, or to which they give their allegiance, but only by concern for the good of all which, moreover, will always be unambiguous and clear to all. All men will be brothers (as brothers are supposed to be). Prophets emerged on the European scene who appealed to

[98]

people in general, or to the working classes in particular, to change or to overthrow the social structure and, through abandonment of private property, to take the road toward the good society.

Karl Marx, while agreeing with the vision of these men, had only scorn for their expectation that their goal, which was also his, could be reached by persuasion and moral exhortation. He called them "utopian" socialists and opposed to their teaching his own "scientific" brand of socialism. He claimed that a cold, "scientific," examination of the human record showed that inexorable laws of history were, in fact, leading men inevitably in this direction. All previous history of man was actually a movement toward the final consummation, the establishment of a classless society, and with it of universal harmony and happiness. Moreover, this goal did not lie in the indefinite future; it was close at hand and after the Russian Revolution, Marxists expected it to be realized within their lifetimes or, at the most, the lifetimes of their children.

In this way, what the heart most eagerly desired, the head declared to be the inevitable outcome of objective laws. Morality was strangely identical with science; *wish and reason conveniently coincided*. The pleasure principle *was* the reality principle.

No wonder that this message has had irresistible appeal to countless people. Perhaps never before in human history has an idea achieved such perfect

[99]

unity between the id, the superego, and a part of
the ego, albeit at an enormous price in terms of
reality testing. When an idea has this kind of appeal, arguments are unlikely to dissuade people
from trying it out, and only prolonged experience
of the actual consequences can bring about dis-
illusionment, at a fearful price in terms of human
suffering.

Socialist realism, in any case, reflects the blend
of moral and scientific (or pseudo-scientific) attitudes characteristic of Marxism, with socialism
representing the moral, and realism the scientific,
component.

The Prospects of the Future

It is impossible to foresee the direction which art
will take in the time to come. The development of
art, as of other fields of activity, depends on a mul-
tiplicity of factors, both of a purely artistic nature
and of the impact of the culture in general, the
power structure, the *Zeitgeist*. In all these respects,
there is a great variety of heterogeneous trends.
We can neither measure nor estimate with any ap-
proximation to accuracy the relative strength of
these trends so as to be able to foresee which ones
will prevail, or to assess the degree to which each
will contribute to the emerging shape of things.
Moreover, the strength of these various trends is
bound to change in an unpredictable fashion under

the impact of the feedback from experience. Under these circumstances it would be idle to speculate about the role that the arts will play or the form they will assume at the end of the century.

But one prediction of a very general nature may perhaps be ventured. The center of the stage in our time is taken by science and technology. The predominant orientation of our time is scientific. Doubts and misgivings in some quarters notwithstanding, most people still take for granted that virtually unlimited horizons of knowledge and of consequent possibilities of control of the human environment have opened up before us and that along this road there lies also the prospect—the only prospect—of universal human happiness, universal human fulfillment, and universal justice. In the first of these assumptions they are most probably right; in the second they are most probably wrong.

Pure science, expanding with tremendous momentum, is teaching us ever more about how things are. But it has offered no answer to the metaphysical question of the purpose of human life and to the moral question of good and evil; and on the answers that men find to these questions—implicit, by living, though not necessarily explicit, in words —depends their conduct of life.

Applied science—technology and medicine—has succeeded beyond all expectations of even the recent past in controlling our physical environment.

[101]

Its achievements make the difference between short lives of hunger, disease, and backbreaking labor, and lives extending over the full Biblical life span, spent in health and vigor, and free from basic wants; only a snob can belittle the magnitude of the achievement. But there are sources of frustration and suffering besides poverty, disease, and premature death. They rest in conditions which cannot, or cannot to any great degree, be controlled and engineered; or if they could be controlled, the issue would immediately arise as to who is going to do the controlling, and in the service of what interests and what ideals. In the beginning was not the Word but the Deed.

Moreover, the absence of severe suffering, while probably for most people a *necessary* condition of happiness, is not at the same time a *sufficient* one; the other condition seems to be a sense of creative achievement.[7]

Applied science has made scant contributions to the latter. It even seems sometimes as though the people of the "affluent society" are often less happy on this score than their hard-struggling parents and grandparents were, for affluence and leisure have brought them face to face, without alibi, with their relative inadequacy; their forebears had all their hands full to keep their heads above water

[7] I am inclined to agree with Jacob Burckhardt's remark that happiness is the absence of suffering, combined with a mild sense of growth.

and in the end they derived a real sense of achievement from the fact that they had pulled through and had raised their families.

But if this is so, the human predicament—or, as it is now usually called, the human "condition"—remains fundamentally the same: the ever-existing possibility of suffering, the constant need for morally responsible decisions in conditions of confusing complexity, the possibility of extreme situations that "try men's souls." And if this is the case, there is likely to remain a place in life for play and for illusion, for contemplation, and for wisdom.

References

Ayrton, M. (1947), The Master of Pastiche. In: *Golden Sections*. London: Methuen.

Benjamin, W. (1936), *Das Kunstwerk in Zeitalter seiner technischen Reproduzierbarkeit*. Frankfurt: Suhrkamp Verlag.

Burckhardt, J. (1868-1871), *Force and Freedom*. New York: Pantheon Books, 1943.

Charbonneaux, J. (1943), *La Sculpture Grèque Classique*. Paris: Fernand Nathan.

Clark, K. (1956), *The Nude: A Study of Ideal Art*. New York: Pantheon Books.

Dirac, P. A. M. (1954), Letter to the *Scientific Monthly*, 79:268-269.

Ferenczi, S. (1919), The Phenomena of Hysterical Materialization. In: *Further Contributions to the Theory and Technique of Psycho-Analysis*. London: Hogarth Press, 1950.

Fremantle, A. & Holme, B. (1954), *Europe: A Journey with Pictures*. New York: Studio Publications & Thomas Y. Crowell.

Freud, S. (1905a), Three Essays on the Theory of Sexuality. *Standard Edition*, 7:125-243. London: Hogarth Press, 1953.

———(1905b), Jokes and Their Relation to the Unconscious. *Standard Edition,* 8. London: Hogarth Press, 1960.

———(1911), Formulations on the Two Principles of Mental Functioning. *Standard Edition,* 12:213-226. London: Hogarth Press, 1958.

———(1913a), Totem and Taboo. *Standard Edition,* 13:1-161. London: Hogarth Press, 1955.

———(1913b), The Claims of Psycho-Analysis to Scientific Interest. *Standard Edition,* 13:165-190. London: Hogarth Press, 1955.

———(1920), Beyond the Pleasure Principle. *Standard Edition,* 18:3-64. London: Hogarth Press, 1955.

———(1924), The Economic Problem of Masochism. *Standard Edition,* 19:157-170. London: Hogarth Press, 1961.

———(1925), An Autobiographical Study. *Standard Edition,* 20:3-74. London: Hogarth Press, 1959.

———(1927a), Humour. *Standard Edition,* 21:159-166. London: Hogarth Press, 1961.

———(1927b), Dostoevsky and Parricide. *Standard Edition,* 21:175-194. London: Hogarth Press, 1961.

———(1933), Preface to Marie Bonaparte's *The Life and Works of Edgar Allen Poe. Standard Edition,* 22:254. London: Hogarth Press, 1964.

George, S., *Poems,* tr. C. N. Vanhope & E. Morwitz. New York: Pantheon Books, 1943.

Gillespie, C. C. (1960), *The Edge of Objectivity.* Princeton: Princeton University Press.

Goethe, J. W., *Faust,* tr. W. Kaufmann. New York: Anchor Books, Doubleday & Co., 1961.

Gombrich, E. R. (1954), Psycho-Analysis and the History of Art. *International Journal of Psycho-Analysis,* 35:401-411.

——(1960), *Art and Illusion.* New York: Pantheon Books.

Kris, E. (1952), *Psychoanalytic Explorations in Art.* New York: International Universities Press.

——& Gombrich, E. R. (1938), The Principles of Caricature. In: *Psychoanalytic Explorations in Art.* New York: International Universities Press, 1952.

——& Kurz, O. (1934), *Die Legende vom Künstler.* Wien: Krystall Verlag.

Landmann, E. (1963), *Gespräche mit Stefan George.* München: Helmut Küpper.

Ortega y Gasset, J. (1948), *The Dehumanisation of Art and Notes on the Novel.* Princeton: Princeton University Press.

Poincaré, H. (1906), *Science and Method,* tr. Francis Maitland. New York: Charles Scribner's Sons, 1916.

Trilling, D. (1964), *Claremont Essays.* New York: Harcourt, Brace & World.

Vercors (1950), Visible-Indivisible [Preface to *L'Art Mediéval Yougoslave*]. *Art et Style,* 15.

Wind, E. (1963), *Art and Anarchy.* London: Faber & Faber.

Wotruba, F. (1945), *Überlegungen, Gedanken zur Kunst.* Zürich: Verlag Oprecht.

Robert Waelder, Ph.D.

Dr. Waelder was born in Vienna in 1900 and received his Ph.D. from the University of Vienna in 1922. From 1925 until 1938 he lectured at the Vienna Psychoanalytic Institute. In 1930 he was awarded a prize by the Deutsche Kant Gesellschaft for a paper on the psychology of faith. From 1930 to 1939 Dr. Waelder and Dr. Ernst Kris were joint editors of *Imago*.

Dr. Waelder came to the United States in 1938 and for the next three years he was a lecturer at the Boston Psychoanalytic Institute. In 1941-1942 he was a lecturer in psychiatric information at Bryn Mawr College. Since 1946 he has been a training and supervising analyst, first with the Philadelphia Psychoanalytic Institute, and then with the Institute of Philadelphia Association for Psychoanalysis. He was President of the Philadelphia Association for Psychoanalysis from 1953 to 1955 and has been Chairman of its Educational Committee from 1955 to 1964. In 1962 Dr. Waelder became Professor of Psychiatry (Psychoanalysis) at Jefferson Medical College in Philadelphia.

Publications by Dr. Waelder

1924

Über Mechanismen und Beeinflussungsmöglichkeiten der Psychosen. *Int. Z. Psa.*, 10:393-414

English: The Psychoses: Their Mechanisms and Accessibility to Influence. *Int. J. Psa.*, 6:259-281, 1925

1925

Über schizophrenes und schöpferisches Denken. *Int. Z. Psa.*, 12:298-308

English: Schizophrenic and Creative Thinking, *Int. J. Psa.*, 7:366-376, 1926

1927

Diskussion der Laienanalyse. *Int. Z. Psa.*, 13:298-299

English: Discussion on Lay Analysis. *Int. J. Psa.*, 8:275-277

1928

Review of: Freud, S., *Hemmung, Symptom und Angst*. *Int. Z. Psa.*, 14:416-423

English: *Int. J. Psa.*, 10:103-111, 1929

1929

Sexualsymbolik bei Naturvölkern. *Psa. Bewegung,* 1:73-75

Die Psychoanalyse im Lebensgefühl des modernen Menschen. *Almanach Psa.,* 47-62

1930

Die latenten metaphysischen Grundlagen der psychologischen Schulen. *Sitzungsber. I. Int. Kongr. ang. Psychopathol. Psychol.,* 178-194

Das Prinzip der mehrfachen Funktion. *Int. Z. Psa.,* 16:286-300

English: The Principle of Multiple Function. *Psa. Quart.,* 5:45-62, 1936

1931

Zeno Cosini von Italo Svevo. *Psa. Bewegung,* 3:170-173

1932

Die psychoanalytische Theorie des Spieles. *Z. psa. Päd.,* 6:184-194; revised version: *Almanach Psa.,* 152-171, 1933

English: The Psychoanalytic Theory of Play, *Psa. Quart.,* 2:208-224, 1933

Review of: Deutsch, H., *Psychoanalyse der Neurosen. Int. Z. Psa.,* 18:125-129

1934

L'Étiologie et l'Évolution des Psychoses Collectives, suivie par quelques Remarques concernant la Situation Historique Actuelle, tr. Marie Bonaparte. In: *L'Esprit, l'Éthique et la Guerre.* Paris:

Institut International de Coopération Intellectuelle (Société des Nations), 3(66):85-150
German: Ätiologie und Verlauf der Massenpsychosen. Mit einen soziologischen Anhang über die geschichtliche Situation der Gegenwart. *Imago*, 21:67-91, 1935
Das Freiheitsproblem in der Psychoanalyse und das Problem der Realitätsprüfung. *Imago*, 20:467-484
English: The Problem of Freedom in Psychoanalysis and the Problem of Reality-Testing. *Int. J. Psa.*, 17:89-108, 1936
Review of: Egyedi, H., *Die Irrtümer der Psychoanalyse*. *Imago*, 20:254

1935

Über den heutigen Stand der Ich-Psychologie. *Int. Z. Psa.*, 21:459-460

1936

Die Bedeutung des Werkes Sigmund Freuds für die Sozial- und Rechtswissenschaften. *Rev. Int. Théorie du Droit*, 10:83-99; also in *Almanach Psa.*, 130-159, 1937
Zur Frage der Genese der psychischen Konflikte im frühen Kindesalter. *Int. Z. Psa.*, 22:513-570
English: The Problem of the Genesis of Psychical Conflicts in Earliest Infancy. *Int. J. Psa.*, 18:406-473, 1937

1938

Kampfmotive und Friedensmotive. *Almanach Psa.*, 103-115

1939

Kriterien der Deutung. *Int. Z. Psa.*, 24:136-145

Psychological Aspects of War and Peace. Geneva: Geneva Research Center

Review of: Kraus, O., *Die Werttheorien. Int. Z. Psa.*, 24:181-182

1940

Democracy and the Scientific Spirit. *Amer. J. Orthopsychiat.*, 10:451-457

Areas of Agreement in Psychotherapy. *Amer. J. Orthopsychiat.*, 10:704-708

1941

(Ed.) *The Living Thoughts of Sigmund Freud.* New York: Longmans, Green

The Scientific Approach to Case Work with Special Emphasis on Psychoanalysis. *Family,* 22:179-185; also in *Personality in Nature, Society and Culture,* ed. C. Kluckhohn & H. A. Murray. New York: Knopf, 1948, 531-539; also in *Principles and Techniques in Social Casework,* ed. C. Casius. New York: Family Service Association

1943

Psychoanalytic Orientation in Family Case Work. *Amer. J. Orthopsychiat.,* 13:2-7

1944

Present Trends in Psychoanalytical Theory and Practice. *Bull. Menninger Clin.,* 8:9-13; also in *The Yearbook of Psychoanalysis,* 1:84-89. New York: International Universities Press, 1945

[114]

1948

Report on Panel Discussion: Mechanisms of Prejudice. *Bull. Amer. Psa. Assn.*, 4(3):7-9

1949

Notes on Prejudice. *Vassar Alumnae Mag.*, 34:2-5, 23-24

Report on Panel Discussion: Dream Theory and Interpretation. *Bull. Amer. Psa. Assn.*, 5(2):36-40

1951

The Structure of Paranoid Ideas: A Critical Survey of Various Theories. *Int. J. Psa.*, 32:167-177

Authoritarianism and Totalitarianism: Psychological Comments on a Problem of Power. In: *Psychoanalysis and Culture,* ed. G. B. Wilbur & W. Muensterberger. New York: International Universities Press, 185-195

Report on Panel Discussion: Problems of Transference and Countertransference. *Bull. Amer. Psa. Assn.*, 6(2):24-27

1952

Psychiatry and the Concept of Criminal Responsibility. *Univ. Penn. Law Rev.*, 101:378-390

1954

Discussion in: Problems of Infantile Neurosis: A Discussion. *The Psychoanalytic Study of the Child,* 9:55-57. New York: International Universities Press.

Discussion in: Problems of Technique in Adult Analysis. *Bull. Phila. Assn. Psa.*, 4:44-69

Discussion of "Considerations Regarding the Loyalty Oath as a Manifestation of Current Social Tension and Anxiety." *G.A.P. Symposium*, 1:19-21

1955

The Functions and the Pitfalls of Psychoanalytic Societies. *Bull. Phila. Assn. Psa.*, 5:1-8

German: Psychoanalytische Gesellschaften; ihre Aufgaben und Gefahren. *Psyche*, 10:677-687

1956

Introduction to the Discussion on Problems of Transference. *Int. J. Psa.*, 37:367-368

Freud and the History of Science. *J. Amer. Psa. Assn.*, 4:602-613

German: Freud und die Geschichte der Wissenschaften. *Psyche*, 11:210-219

Critical Discussion of the Concept of an Instinct of Destruction. *Bull. Phila. Assn. Psa.*, 6:97-109

1958

Neurotic Ego Distortion: Opening Remarks to the Panel Discussion. *Int. J. Psa.*, 39:243-244

Discussion Remarks to: Freud, Anna, Child Observation and Prediction of Development. *The Psychoanalytic Study of the Child*, 13:123-124. New York: International Universities Press

1959

A Hypothesis about the Nature of an Archaic Society. *World Politics*, 12:92-102

1960

Basic Theory of Psychoanalysis. New York: International Universities Press

French: *Les Fondements de la Psychanalyse.* Paris: Payot, 1962

German: *Die Grundlagen der Psychoanalyse.* Bern: Huber; Stuttgart: Klett, 1963

The Psychoanalytic Theory of the Neuroses: An Outline. In: *Current Approaches to Psychoanalysis,* ed. P. H. Hoch & J. Zubin. New York: Grune & Stratton

Characteristics of Totalitarianism. *The Psychoanalytic Study of Society,* 1:11-25. New York: International Universities Press

1962

Demoralization and Re-education. *World Politics,* 14: 375-385

Psychoanalysis, Scientific Method, and Philosophy. *J. Amer. Psa. Assn.,* 10:617-637

Protest and Revolt against Western Societies. In: *Revolution in World Politics,* ed. M. A. Kaplan. New York: Wiley, 3-27

Symposium: Selection Criteria for the Training of Psycho-Analytic Students. *Int. J. Psa.,* 43:283-286

1963

Psychic Determinism and the Possibility of Predictions. *Psa. Quart.* 32:15-42

Historical Fiction. *J. Amer. Psa. Assn.,* 11:628-651

1964

Civil Disobedience. *Jewish Exponent,* July

[117]

PUBLICATIONS BY DR. WAELDER

1965

Progress and Revolution
A Study of the Issues of Our Age (in press)

[118]

Name Index

The Freud Anniversary Lecture Series
The New York Psychoanalytic Institute

Previously published volumes

FREUD: MAN AND SCIENTIST

By *Rudolph M. Loewenstein*

DREAMS AND THE USES OF REGRESSION

By *Bertram D. Lewin*

A GENETIC FIELD THEORY OF EGO FORMATION:
ITS IMPLICATIONS FOR PATHOLOGY

By *René A. Spitz*

PSYCHOANALYSIS AND MORAL VALUES

By *Heinz Hartmann*

THE PSYCHOANALYTIC SITUATION: AN EXAMINA-
TION OF ITS DEVELOPMENT AND ESSENTIAL
NATURE

By *Leo Stone*

[121]

THE QUEST FOR THE FATHER: A STUDY OF THE DARWIN-BUTLER CONTROVERSY, AS A CONTRIBUTION TO THE UNDERSTANDING OF THE CREATIVE INDIVIDUAL

By *Phyllis Greenacre*